also by america's test kitchen

praise for other america's test kitchen titles

"If there's room in the budget for one multicooker/Instant Pot cookbook, make it this one."
BOOKLIST ON *MULTICOOKER PERFECTION*

"This book begins with a detailed buying guide, a critical summary of available sizes and attachments, and a list of clever food processor techniques. Easy and versatile dishes follow. . . . Both new and veteran food processor owners will love this practical guide."
LIBRARY JOURNAL ON *FOOD PROCESSOR PERFECTION*

"This book upgrades slow cooking for discriminating, 21st-century palates—that is indeed revolutionary."
THE DALLAS MORNING NEWS ON *SLOW COOKER REVOLUTION*

"A terrifically accessible and useful guide to grilling in all its forms that sets a new bar for its competitors on the bookshelf. . . . The book is packed with practical advice, simple tips, and approachable recipes."
PUBLISHERS WEEKLY (STARRED REVIEW) ON *MASTER OF THE GRILL*

"This encyclopedia of meat cookery would feel completely overwhelming if it weren't so meticulously organized and artfully designed. This is Cook's Illustrated at its finest."
THE KITCHN ON *THE COOK'S ILLUSTRATED MEAT BOOK*

Selected as one of the 10 Best New Cookbooks of 2017
THE LA TIMES ON *THE PERFECT COOKIE*

"With 1,000 photos and the expertise of the America's Test Kitchen editors, this title might be the definitive book on bread baking."
PUBLISHERS WEEKLY ON *BREAD ILLUSTRATED*

Selected as the Cookbook Award Winner of 2019 in the Health and Special Diet Category
INTERNATIONAL ASSOCIATION OF CULINARY PROFESSIONALS (IACP) ON *THE COMPLETE DIABETES COOKBOOK*

"If you're a home cook who loves long introductions that tell you why a dish works followed by lots of step-by-step hand holding, then you'll love *Vegetables Illustrated*."
THE WALL STREET JOURNAL ON *VEGETABLES ILLUSTRATED*

Selected as one of Amazon's Best Books of 2015 in the Cookbooks and Food Writing Category
AMAZON ON *THE COMPLETE VEGETARIAN COOKBOOK*

"The 21st-century *Fannie Farmer Cookbook* or *The Joy of Cooking*. If you had to have one cookbook and that's all you could have, this one would do it."
CBS SAN FRANCISCO ON *THE NEW FAMILY COOKBOOK*

"The go-to gift book for newlyweds, small families, or empty nesters."
ORLANDO SENTINEL ON *THE COMPLETE COOKING FOR TWO COOKBOOK*

"The sum total of exhaustive experimentation . . . anyone interested in gluten-free cookery simply shouldn't be without it."
NIGELLA LAWSON ON *THE HOW CAN IT BE GLUTEN-FREE COOKBOOK*

"A one-volume kitchen seminar, addressing in one smart chapter after another the sometimes surprising whys behind a cook's best practices. . . . You get the myth, the theory, the science, and the proof, all rigorously interrogated as only America's Test Kitchen can do."
NPR ON *THE SCIENCE OF GOOD COOKING*

"The perfect kitchen home companion. . . . The practical side of things is very much on display . . . cook-friendly and kitchen-oriented, illuminating the process of preparing food instead of mystifying it."
THE WALL STREET JOURNAL ON *THE COOK'S ILLUSTRATED COOKBOOK*

MEDITERRANEAN
INSTANT POT®

Easy, Inspired Meals for Eating Well

AMERICA'S TEST KITCHEN

Library of Congress Cataloging-in-Publication
Data has been applied for.

ISBN 978-1-948703-06-2

AMERICA'S
TEST KITCHEN ®

AMERICA'S TEST KITCHEN
21 Drydock Avenue, Boston, MA 02210

Manufactured in the United States of America

10 9 8 7 6 5 4 3 2 1

Distributed by Penguin Random House
Publisher Services
Tel: 800.733.3000

pictured on front cover
Sicilian Fish Stew (page 35)

pictured on back cover
Braised Whole Cauliflower with
North African Spices (page 171)

editorial director, books Adam Kowit

executive food editor Dan Zuccarello

executive managing editor Debra Hudak

senior editors Joseph Gitter, Nicole Konstantinakos,
and Russell Selander

associate editor Lawman Johnson

assistant editors Kelly Cormier and Brenna Donovan

art director, books Lindsey Timko Chandler

deputy art director Allison Boales

associate art director Katie Barranger

photography director Julie Bozzo Cote

photography producer Meredith Mulcahy

senior staff photographers Steve Klise and
Daniel J. van Ackere

staff photographer Kevin White

additional photography Keller + Keller

food styling Catrine Kelty, Chantal Lambeth,
Ashley Moore, Elle Simone Scott, and Kendra Smith

photoshoot kitchen team

    photo team manager Timothy McQuinn

    assistant test cooks Sarah Ewald, Hannah Fenton,
    Jacqueline Gochenouer, and Eric Haessler

senior manager, publishing operations
Taylor Argenzio

imaging manager Lauren Robbins

production and imaging specialists
Tricia Neumyer, Dennis Noble,
Jessica Voas, and Amanda Yong

copy editor Jeffrey Schier

proofreader Ann-Marie Imbornoni

indexer Elizabeth Parson

chief creative officer Jack Bishop

executive editorial directors
Julia Collin Davison and
Bridget Lancaster

contents

welcome to america's test kitchen

This book has been tested, written, and edited by the folks at America's Test Kitchen. Located in Boston's Seaport District in the historic Innovation and Design Building, it features 15,000 square feet of kitchen space including multiple photography and video studios. It is the home of *Cook's Illustrated* magazine and *Cook's Country* magazine and is the workday destination for more than 60 test cooks, editors, and cookware specialists. Our mission is to test recipes over and over again until we understand how and why they work and until we arrive at the best version. Our television show highlights the absolute best recipes developed in the test kitchen during the past year—those recipes that our test kitchen staff makes at home time and time again. These recipes are accompanied by our most exhaustive equipment tests and our most interesting food tastings.

We start the process of testing a recipe with a complete lack of preconceptions, which means that we accept no claim, no technique, and no recipe at face value. We simply assemble as many variations as possible, test a half-dozen of the most promising, and taste the results blind. We then construct our own recipe and continue to test it, varying ingredients, techniques, and cooking times until we reach a consensus. As we like to say in the test kitchen, "We make the mistakes so you don't have to." The result, we hope, is the best version of a particular recipe, but we realize that only you can be the final judge of our success (or failure). We use the same rigorous approach when we test equipment and taste ingredients.

All of this would not be possible without a belief that good cooking, much like good music, is based on a foundation of objective technique. Some people like spicy foods and others don't, but there is a right way to sauté, there is a best way to cook a pot roast, and there are measurable scientific principles involved in producing perfectly beaten, stable egg whites.

Our ultimate goal is to investigate the fundamental principles of cooking to give you the techniques, tools, and ingredients you need to become a better cook. It is as simple as that.

To see what goes on behind the scenes at America's Test Kitchen, check out our social media channels for kitchen snapshots, exclusive content, video tips, and much more. You can watch us work (in our actual test kitchen) by tuning in to *America's Test Kitchen* or *Cook's Country* on public television or on our websites. Download our award-winning podcast *Proof*, which goes beyond recipes to solve food mysteries (AmericasTestKitchen.com/proof), or listen in to test kitchen experts on public radio (SplendidTable.org) to hear insights that illuminate the truth about real home cooking. Want to hone your cooking skills or finally learn how to bake—with an America's Test Kitchen test cook? Enroll in one of our online cooking classes. And you can engage the next generation of home cooks with kid-tested recipes from America's Test Kitchen Kids.

However you choose to visit us, we welcome you into our kitchen, where you can stand by our side as we test our way to the best recipes in America.

facebook.com/AmericasTestKitchen
twitter.com/TestKitchen
youtube.com/AmericasTestKitchen
instagram.com/TestKitchen
pinterest.com/TestKitchen

AmericasTestKitchen.com
CooksIllustrated.com
CooksCountry.com
OnlineCookingSchool.com
AmericasTestKitchen.com/kids

getting started

introduction

The test kitchen has long extolled the virtues of the Mediterranean way of eating. With its emphasis on whole grains, vegetables, and heart-healthy olive oil and fish, it has become a diet in its own right, and countless studies have shown that its benefits go far beyond deliciousness.

A Mediterranean meal often comprises multiple smaller dishes, but when you're trying to get dinner on the table the last thing you want is to be tied to the stove. Enter: the Instant Pot. This little appliance helps you achieve healthy, hands-off weeknight meals, whether it's cooking dried beans to the perfect tender consistency or executing a top-notch tagine on a Tuesday.

When we set out to develop our recipes, we had some requirements. First, we wanted to take the multiple-dish mentality and translate it into easy-to-execute one-pot meals. Instead of juggling countless elements, all of our recipes are a complete meal. Second, we didn't want to overcomplicate things. The meals are simple to prepare yet still jam-packed with flavor and good-for-you ingredients.

Many Instant Pot recipes are heavy red-meat-centered dishes more fit for a New England snowstorm than for springtime on the Amalfi Coast. We show off the lighter, more vibrant side of the Instant Pot. In the pages that follow you'll find exhaustively tested recipes for Mediterranean-inspired meals like Swordfish with Peppers and Potatoes, and Lamb Meatballs with Couscous, Pickled Onions, and Tahini. We also help you become a meal prep maven with charts that detail cook times for rice and grains, dried beans and lentils, vegetables, and proteins. We show you how to create a beautiful meze spread using your Instant Pot, and how to build a DIY Mediterranean pantry complete with sauces and finishing elements to accompany your pressure-cooked dishes, from Classic Basil Pesto to Za'atar.

Best of all? We help you take full advantage of the Mediterranean diet while also saving valuable time and effort—almost all of the recipes in this book take you from cutting board to plate (or bowl) in under an hour. Here's to an easier, quicker way to eat well.

across the mediterranean in an instant

So what does it mean to follow a Mediterranean diet? The Mediterranean Sea is surrounded by an extraordinarily diverse group of countries, which means that there isn't a single "diet." Rather, the Mediterranean diet is about what these cuisines have in common: a daily emphasis on fresh vegetables and fruits, beans and lentils, whole grains, seafood more than meat and poultry, and olive oil.

Following a Mediterranean diet has been proven to be one of the healthiest ways to eat. In this book we wholeheartedly endorse the tenets of the Mediterranean way of eating while also taking simplifying liberties with the busy home cook in mind, rather than adhering strictly to authentic ingredients and methods. For example, you won't find salmon swimming in the Mediterranean, but we included it because it is popular and widely available in the United States, and it is brimming with heart-healthy fat.

There is no denying that eating the Mediterranean way requires a shift in thinking: A lesser amount of meat defines a serving size, and meals are often built around whole grains and vegetables. Flavoring comes from potent spices and fresh herbs, and you won't find butter in these recipes (in fact, dairy itself is used sparingly, and often in the form of yogurt or small amounts of cheeses).

Our goal was to make this shift easier for you. By creating one-pot meals that adhere to the Mediterranean diet, we took care of the heavy lifting of meal planning. We used the guidelines that follow when developing our recipes.

everything in moderation
Portions are smaller in the Mediterranean diet. That's why our recipes call for pieces of chicken and meat in the 4- to 6-ounce range, or use meat more as a flavoring element. A little bit of ground chicken, for example, goes a long way in flavoring our Couscous with Chicken, Fennel, and Peppers.

opt for beans and whole grains
Since red meat and poultry are used more sparingly in the Mediterranean, beans, lentils, nuts, and whole grains are included to round out meals.

eat more lean proteins
Seafood is a major component of the Mediterranean diet, and it is often the main source of protein.

spice it up
Because the Mediterranean diet uses less salt, fresh herbs and potent spices are added to boost flavor.

using your instant pot

We developed the recipes for this book using the Instant Pot because it is the most widely owned electric pressure cooker. Pressure cookers are finicky machines—just 1 minute too long can turn a succulent piece of fish into a rubbery disappointment, or cause beans to burst open into a gloppy mess. So we standardized our recipes to ensure we were precise with our timing. All of the recipes in this book were designed to work in both the Duo and the Ultra models, as well as in the 6-quart and 8-quart sizes. If you own a different brand of electric pressure cooker, note that cook times will vary.

what's happening?

In a tightly sealed pot under pressure, the boiling point of liquid is higher. Under normal conditions, water boils and turns to steam at 212 degrees Fahrenheit. In a closed environment, however, the water molecules can't escape, increasing the pressure in the pot. More energy is needed for the water to boil, so the temperature in the pot increases. This means that you are cooking food with steam that's at a temperature up to 34 degrees higher than what's possible in a normal pot, which translates to shorter cooking times.

high pressure versus low pressure

The Instant Pot has two pressure levels: high and low. Most recipes in this book use high pressure since it is the most efficient. (It is the *Instant* Pot, after all.) We used low pressure for some bean recipes where the texture was paramount, like our Cannellini Bean Salad.

natural release versus quick release

There are two methods to release pressure after cooking. The one you use will affect the final outcome of a recipe—so don't swap one for the other. Most important, don't force the Instant Pot open before the pressure has been fully released.

natural release

If you do nothing or turn off the pot when the cooking time ends, the Instant Pot will allow the pressure in the pot to drop back down naturally. This is the preferred method when you want to gently finish cooking food through, since it will continue to cook as the pressure drops. A natural release can also affect texture: If you quickly release the pressure on our Braised Short Ribs with Fennel and Pickled Grapes, for example, the meat will seize up and be tough. Our method was to quick-release any remaining pressure after 15 minutes of natural release.

quick release

You can immediately release pressure by turning the pressure regulator knob to "steam" as soon as your recipe is done cooking. Be careful—the steam will be hot. We usually use a quick release when we want to stop the cooking right away because the food can easily overcook (think delicate fish).

tips for success

While we love that the Instant Pot eliminates the need for multiple cooking vessels, there were a few tools we reached for time and time again when developing recipes for this book.

keep a meat thermometer handy Don't guess at meat and fish doneness when developing your own recipes. Temp your proteins after releasing pressure.

reach for tongs The Instant Pot is narrow, so we preferred tongs over unwieldy spatulas as our primary flipping tool.

towel your grain pilafs The secret to fluffy, distinct grains is putting a dish towel under the lid after cooking and letting the contents rest, allowing excess moisture in the pot to be absorbed.

use your own timer The Instant Pot's timer can be hard to hear, so we recommend using a kitchen timer to keep track of cooking time, especially for quick-cooking foods like Soft-Cooked Eggs.

measure up For even cooking, it's crucial to make sure all ingredients are the exact dimensions called for in the recipe. Use a ruler to ensure everything from salmon fillets to fennel is the proper thickness.

layer pots Use a 1½-quart round soufflé dish to cook separate components without dirtying the inner cooking pot, or for dishes that need a gentler hand, like polenta.

---

use a foil sling for more control

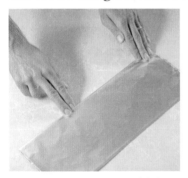  

making a foil sling Fold sheet of aluminum foil into 16 by 6-inch rectangle by folding either in half or in thirds, depending on width of foil.

using a foil sling for fish Arrange fish in center of sling, on top of lemons if called for. Using sling, lower fish into pot; allow narrow edges of sling to rest along sides of insert.

using a foil sling for a soufflé dish For polenta, rest 1½-quart round soufflé dish in center of sling. Using sling, lower dish into pot and onto trivet; allow narrow edges of sling to rest along sides of insert.

troubleshooting

In the test kitchen, we embrace setbacks, because they bring us closer to achieving foolproof recipes. After spending months in the kitchen with our Instant Pots, we came up with a few key tricks to fix the common problems we encountered.

problem	solution	notes
undercooked food	Continue to cook the food using the highest sauté function	Since it's impossible to test the doneness of food as it cooks under pressure, sometimes food might be slightly underdone. Simply finish cooking by partially covering the pot, switching to the highest sauté function, and adding extra liquid as needed.
uneven cooking	Prep ingredients as directed	There's no going back on an unevenly cooked dish, but to ensure the best results next time, be sure that your ingredients are prepped properly: Buy fish within the thickness range we call for, measure liquids accurately, and grab a ruler when prepping vegetables. Arranging the ingredients in an even layer also helps safeguard against unevenness.
sauce is too thick, or too thin	Add more liquid, or continue to simmer (or let it rest)	Sauces that are too thin can be simmered uncovered on the highest sauté function to thicken up before serving, and thick sauces can be thinned out with additional broth or water. Keep in mind that many dishes may look a little watery when you open the lid, but a brief rest allows them to thicken up.
scorching during cooking	Add additional liquid and scrape up browned bits	We made sure that the recipes in this book contain enough liquid to prevent scorching, but keep an eye out when using your own recipes. If you find that food is burning while you're sautéing, try adding a small amount of liquid to slow down the cooking. Although you can't fix food that has been burned during pressure cooking, you can avoid the problem in the future by taking care to scrape up all the browned bits left in the pot after sautéing food and before closing the lid. An improperly sealed lid can also cause the Instant Pot to continue to release steam as it attempts to reach pressure, and this will lead to scorching.
never reaching pressure	Check the silicone gasket and pressure regulating knob	If your Instant Pot is not coming to pressure, it may not be sealed correctly. Check that the silicone gasket around the bottom lip of the lid is not cracked or improperly installed, and make sure that the pressure regulating knob (located on the lid) is in the closed position.
burn message	Depressurize and inspect; add liquid	This is an indication of overheating. When a high temperature is detected at the bottom of the inner pot, the burn-protection mechanism suspends heating to avoid burning food. In denser dishes like rice and grains, or in dishes with thicker sauces, sometimes the available liquid is pushed to the top while the solids settle to the bottom, causing overheating. Stir to recombine or add more liquid if necessary.

cooking rice and grains

The Instant Pot is a convenient way to cook big batches of your favorite rice and grains, and it makes it easy to explore new whole grains. It's simple to jazz them up by stirring in olive oil, fresh herbs, a splash of lemon juice or vinegar, or other flavorful ingredients such as olives, chopped sun-dried tomatoes, toasted nuts, and/or grated Parmesan.

what we learned

rinse rice and grains Grains and rice are typically coated with a thin dusting of starch. This coating needs to be rinsed away before cooking or else the rice/grains clump together, and the cooking water turns starchy and foamy, potentially causing the pressure valve to clog. To rinse your rice and grains, place them in a fine-mesh strainer set under running water and stir with your hand until the water runs clear. (The exceptions for this rule are recipes where we want the starch to help thicken the dish, like risotto.)

always add a little oil Adding oil when cooking both rice and grains helps the individual grains remain more distinct and clump less. Oil also helps reduce the amount of starchy foam.

use enough water Having enough water in the pot proved crucial for even cooking. We use the boil method for heartier grains that can withstand a more vigorous cooking process. The amount also affects the time it takes for the pot to come to pressure and the cooking time; don't be tempted to adjust the water amounts.

the pressure release type matters
We generally prefer a natural release for most rice and grains, but we use the quick release method for grains with shorter cook times. Keep in mind that release types and cooking times go hand in hand; don't be tempted to swap release types as it will dramatically affect the results.

cooking instructions

for pilaf method Rinse 1½ cups rice/grains, then combine with water, 1 tablespoon oil, and ½ teaspoon salt in Instant Pot. Lock lid in place and close pressure release valve. Select high pressure cook function and cook for time listed in chart. Turn off Instant Pot and release pressure as directed in chart. Carefully remove lid, allowing steam to escape away from you. Gently fluff rice/grains with fork. Lay clean dish towel over pot, replace lid, and let sit for 5 minutes. Makes about 4 cups.

for boil method Rinse 1½ cups rice/grains, then combine with water, 1 tablespoon oil, and 1½ teaspoons salt in Instant Pot. (When cooking wheat berries reduce salt to ½ teaspoon.) Lock lid in place and close pressure release valve. Select high pressure cook function and cook for time listed in chart. Turn off Instant Pot and let pressure release as directed. Carefully remove lid, allowing steam to escape away from you. Drain cooked rice/grains through fine-mesh strainer. Makes about 4 cups.

make-ahead

All of these can be cooked, cooled, and refrigerated in an airtight container for up to 3 days. To reheat, microwave in covered bowl until hot, fluffing with fork halfway through microwaving, then season to taste (reheating time will vary depending on the quantity and type of rice or grains used).

rice/grain	cooking method	water amount	cook time	release type
long-grain white rice	pilaf	2 cups	4 minutes	quick
long-grain brown rice	pilaf	2⅓ cups	12 minutes	natural
wild rice	boil	6 cups	15 minutes	natural
wheat berries	boil	6 cups	30 minutes	natural
farro	boil	6 cups	8 minutes	quick
pearled barley	boil	6 cups	8 minutes	natural
bulgur (medium-grind)	pilaf	2⅓ cups	1 minute	quick
cracked freekeh	pilaf	1¾ cups	4 minutes	quick
whole freekeh	boil	6 cups	15 minutes	natural

no-stir parmesan polenta
serves 4

Coarse-ground degerminated cornmeal such as yellow grits (with uniform grains the size of couscous) works best in this recipe. Avoid instant or quick-cooking products, as well as whole-grain, stone-ground, or regular cornmeal. You will need a 1½-quart round soufflé dish or ceramic dish of similar size for this recipe.

1 cup coarse-ground cornmeal
¼ teaspoon table salt
2 ounces Parmesan cheese, grated (1 cup)

1 Arrange trivet included with Instant Pot in base of insert and add 1 cup water. Fold sheet of aluminum foil into 16 by 6-inch sling, then rest 1½-quart round soufflé dish in center of sling. Whisk water, cornmeal, and salt together in dish. Using sling, lower dish into pot and onto trivet; allow narrow edges of sling to rest along sides of insert.

2 Lock lid in place and close pressure release valve. Select high pressure cook function and cook for 40 minutes. Turn off Instant Pot and quick-release pressure. Carefully remove lid, allowing steam to escape away from you.

3 Using sling, transfer soufflé dish to wire rack; remove trivet. Whisk Parmesan into polenta, smoothing out any lumps, and let sit until thickened slightly, about 10 minutes. Season polenta with salt and pepper to taste.

cooking beans and lentils

We prefer the flavor and texture of dried beans to canned, and the Instant Pot proves itself truly invaluable here since it can cook dried beans (and lentils) in a fraction of their conventional cooking time.

what we learned

brine beans before cooking Brining beans before cooking is crucial for even cooking and to minimize busted beans (it's not necessary to brine lentils). If you have time, brine your beans overnight (or up to 24 hours) in a combination of 2 quarts cold water and 1½ tablespoons salt. If you are pressed for time, you can "quick-brine" your beans. Combine the water, salt, and beans in your Instant Pot. Bring the mixture to boil using the highest sauté function, then turn off the Instant Pot and let the beans sit for 1 hour. Drain and rinse the beans well before proceeding with the cooking instructions.

always add a little oil Adding oil to the cooking liquid prevents foaming.

use natural release (usually) We generally prefer a natural release for beans, but we use the quick release method for beans that are in danger of overcooking.

skim the floaters Sometimes we notice a few beans floating on top of the water after releasing the pressure and removing the lid. These beans typically turn out underdone, so it's best to fish them out of the pot.

cooking instructions

Add 1 pound beans that have been brined or 2 cups lentils, 8 cups water, 1 tablespoon extra-virgin olive oil, and ½ teaspoon salt to Instant Pot. Lock lid in place and close pressure release valve. Select low pressure cook function and cook for amount of time listed in chart. Turn off Instant Pot and let pressure release as directed. Skim any beans or lentils floating on top of water and discard. Drain cooked beans or lentils through fine-mesh strainer.

bean type	cook time	release type
black-eyed peas	3 minutes	quick
cannellini beans	3 minutes	quick
chickpeas	6 minutes	natural
gigante beans	7 minutes	natural
great northern beans	2 minutes	quick
pinto beans	3 minutes	quick
French green lentils (lentilles du Puy)	0 minutes*	natural
brown/green lentils	7 minutes	quick

*As soon as pressure is reached, turn off Instant Pot.

cooking vegetables

While the previous charts were more meal prep–focused, these times are a summary of the testing that we did for this book, and they served as our guidelines when developing recipes. This chart is meant to give you general cooking times as you build your own recipes. These times (with quick pressure release) are just a starting point, and can vary depending on how you cut the vegetables and what else you add to the Instant Pot. Note that you will need to add a minimum of ½ cup of liquid for the pot to reach pressure, but this too can vary.

vegetable	cook time
1½ pounds **baby artichokes**, stemmed, leaf tips trimmed, halved	3 minutes
1½ pounds whole **artichokes**, stemmed, top quarter removed, leaf tips trimmed	10 minutes
1½ pounds unpeeled **beets**, scrubbed, trimmed, and cut into ½-inch wedges	8 minutes
1½ pounds **butternut squash**, peeled, seeded, and cut into 1-inch pieces	6 minutes
1½ pounds **eggplant**, cut into 1-inch pieces	1 minute
1½ pounds **green** or **red cabbage**, cored and sliced 1 inch thick	3 minutes
1½ pounds **carrots**, peeled and cut into 3-inch lengths, larger pieces halved lengthwise	1 minute
1½ pounds **celery root**, peeled and cut into 1-inch pieces	5 minutes
1½ pounds **cauliflower**, cored and cut into 2-inch florets	0 minutes*
1½ pounds **fennel**, stalks discarded, bulbs halved, each half cut into 1-inch-thick wedges	2 minutes
1½ pounds **kale**, stemmed and cut into 1-inch pieces	3 minutes
1½ pounds **radishes**, trimmed and quartered	1 minute
1½ pounds **red** or **Yukon Gold potatoes**, unpeeled, cut into 1-inch pieces	8 minutes
1½ pounds **zucchini**, halved lengthwise and sliced 1 inch thick	1 minute

*As soon as pressure is reached, turn off Instant Pot.

cooking proteins

As is the case with the vegetables chart, these times are just a starting point and are meant to give you general cooking times as you build your own recipes. These times can vary depending on what else you add to the Instant Pot. Note that you will need to add a minimum of ½ cup of liquid for the pot to reach pressure, but this too can vary.

what we learned

seafood is successful We were pleasantly surprised to find that the Instant Pot yielded such moist and succulent fish. But you have to be careful—focusing on thickness rather than weight is key, as thinner pieces tend to dry out quicker. A foil sling (page 4) makes for easy removal from the pot.

browning adds flavor But it isn't always necessary! For potently spiced dishes like Chicken Tagine, we could skip the browning step, but we found it added depth of flavor for simpler dishes like Lemony Chicken with Fingerling Potatoes and Olives. And we loved that it could be done using the Instant Pot's sauté function.

sync up cook times Because we were creating complete meals, we took care to pair the right proteins with other elements that cooked in a similar amount of time. That perfectly cooked chicken breast will do you no good if it's paired with crunchy, undercooked rice.

finish with bright elements The Instant Pot tends to dull flavors (we had to add a much greater amount of spices than when using the stovetop), so drizzling the finished dish with a lemony sauce or sprinkling it with fresh herbs helps to wake everything up.

hard-cooked eggs
serves 4
This recipe can be doubled; do not increase the water amount.

> 4 large eggs

Arrange trivet included with Instant Pot in base of insert and add 1 cup water. Using highest sauté function, bring water to boil. Set eggs on trivet. Lock lid in place and close pressure release valve. Select high pressure cook function and cook for 8 minutes. Turn off Instant Pot and quick-release pressure. Carefully remove lid, allowing steam to escape away from you. Using tongs, transfer eggs to bowl of ice water and let sit for 15 minutes. Peel before using.

soft-cooked eggs
We recommend using a kitchen timer to track the cook time once the Instant Pot has reached pressure.

Follow directions above, but reduce pressure cook time to 2½ minutes for fully set whites with runny yolks, or 3 minutes for fully set whites with fudgy yolks. Place eggs under cold running water for 30 seconds before peeling.

protein	cook time	release type
fish and shellfish		
4 (6-ounce) skinless **salmon fillets**, about 1½ inches thick	3 minutes	quick
4 (6-ounce) skinless **cod, haddock,** or **hake fillets**, about 1½ inches thick	3 minutes	quick
4 (6-ounce) skinless **halibut, striped bass,** or **swordfish fillets**, about 1½ inches thick	0 minutes*	quick
2 pounds **littleneck clams**, scrubbed	1 minute	quick
3 pounds **mussels**, scrubbed and debearded	0 minutes*	quick
poultry		
2 (12-ounce) bone-in split **chicken breasts**, trimmed	4 minutes	quick
4 (5- to 7-ounce) bone-in **chicken thighs**, trimmed	10 minutes	quick
meat		
1½ pounds boneless **chuck-eye roast**, trimmed and cut into 2-inch pieces	35 minutes	natural
1½ pounds boneless **beef short ribs**, trimmed and cut into 2-inch pieces	35 minutes	natural
2 pounds bone-in **English-style beef short ribs**, trimmed	60 minutes	natural
4 (8- to 10-ounce) bone-in **blade-cut pork chops**, about ¾ inch thick, trimmed	10 minutes	natural
1½ pounds boneless **pork butt roast**, trimmed and cut into 3-inch pieces	30 minutes	natural
4 (8- to 12-ounce) **lamb shoulder chops** (round bone or blade), about ¾ inch thick	20 minutes	natural
4 (10- to 12-ounce) **lamb shanks**, trimmed	60 minutes	natural

*As soon as pressure is reached, turn off Instant Pot.

DIY mediterranean pantry

Whether you want to put together a company-worthy meze spread or
brighten up a completed dish with a homemade sauce or finishing element,
we've got you covered. These recipes are referenced throughout the book,
but they can also be utilized beyond your Instant Pot meals.

meze

hummus

makes about 2 cups

To serve with pita chips and crudités, we like to spread the hummus in a shallow bowl, then drizzle with extra-virgin olive oil and sprinkle with toasted sesame seeds, ground dried Aleppo pepper, and/or chopped fresh parsley.

 2 teaspoons table salt, for brining
 8 ounces (1¼ cups) dried chickpeas, picked over and rinsed
 1 tablespoon extra-virgin olive oil
1¼ teaspoons table salt, divided
 ½ cup lemon juice (3 lemons)
 4 garlic cloves, unpeeled
 ⅔ cup tahini
 ¼ teaspoon ground cumin

1 Dissolve 2 teaspoons salt in 4 cups cold water in large bowl. Add chickpeas and soak at room temperature for at least 8 hours or up to 24 hours. Drain and rinse well.

2 Add chickpeas, 2 cups water, oil, and ¼ teaspoon salt to Instant Pot. Lock lid in place and close pressure release valve. Select high pressure cook function and cook for 15 minutes.

3 Turn off Instant Pot and quick-release pressure. Carefully remove lid, allowing steam to escape away from you. Drain beans, reserving ⅓ cup cooking liquid, and set aside.

4 Pulse reserved cooking liquid, lemon juice, garlic, and remaining 1 teaspoon salt in food processor until coarse puree forms, about 20 pulses. Transfer to small bowl and let steep for 10 minutes. Strain lemon juice mixture through fine-mesh strainer back into processor; discard solids.

Add tahini and process until mixture is smooth and well combined, about 1 minute, scraping down sides of bowl as needed. Add beans and cumin and process until mixture is very smooth, about 4 minutes. Adjust consistency with up to 2 tablespoons water, and season with salt to taste. (Hummus can be refrigerated for up to 3 days. Let sit at room temperature for 30 minutes before serving.)

baba ghanoush

makes about 2 cups

Creamy eggplant, bright lemon juice, and nutty tahini shine in this Middle Eastern staple.

 3 tablespoons extra-virgin olive oil, divided, plus extra for drizzling
 1 onion, cut into 1-inch pieces
 2 pounds eggplant, peeled and cut into 2-inch pieces
 1 cup chicken or vegetable broth
 2 tablespoons tahini
 4 teaspoons lemon juice
 1 small garlic clove, minced
 ¾ teaspoon table salt
 ¼ teaspoon pepper
 2 teaspoons chopped fresh parsley

1 Using highest sauté function, heat 1 tablespoon oil in Instant Pot until shimmering. Add onion and cook until softened and lightly browned, 5 to 7 minutes. Add eggplant and broth. Lock lid in place and close pressure release valve. Select high pressure cook function and cook for 6 minutes.

2 Turn off Instant Pot and quick-release pressure. Carefully remove lid, allowing steam to escape away from you. Set colander over bowl. Using slotted spoon, transfer eggplant and onion to colander and let drain for 3 minutes.

3 Transfer drained vegetables to food processor. Add remaining 2 tablespoons oil, tahini, lemon juice, garlic, salt, and pepper. Pulse mixture to coarse puree, about 8 pulses, scraping down sides of bowl as needed.

4 Transfer baba ghanoush to serving bowl, cover, and refrigerate until chilled, about 1 hour. Season with salt and pepper to taste. Drizzle with extra oil and sprinkle with parsley before serving. (Dip can be refrigerated for up to 24 hours; bring to room temperature before serving.)

homemade yogurt
makes about 4 cups

The success of this recipe hinges on using yogurt that contains live and active cultures. The longer the yogurt cooks, the tangier it will be.

3½ cups whole milk
¼ cup plain yogurt with live and
   active cultures

1 Add milk to Instant Pot and, using highest sauté function, bring to 185 degrees. Turn off Instant Pot and strain milk through fine-mesh strainer into 8-cup liquid measuring cup. Let milk cool until it registers 110 degrees, stirring occasionally to prevent skin from forming, about 30 minutes.

2 Combine yogurt and ½ cup cooled milk in small bowl. Gently stir yogurt mixture into remaining cooled milk, then transfer to two 16-ounce Mason jars and seal; do not overtighten lids.

3 Place trivet included with Instant Pot in clean insert and add water until it reaches base of trivet. Place jars on trivet. Lock lid in place and open pressure release valve. Select normal yogurt function and cook for 6 to 18 hours.

4 Turn off Instant Pot and carefully remove lid, allowing steam to escape away from you. Carefully remove jars and let yogurt cool at room temperature for 15 minutes. Transfer to refrigerator and let sit until fully chilled, about 3 hours. Stir yogurt to recombine before serving. (Yogurt can be refrigerated for up to 1 week; stir to recombine before serving.)

yogurt cheese
makes about 1 cup

Thick, rich, and spreadable, this snack is the star of any meze spread. We prefer to use our Homemade Yogurt here; however, you can substitute store-bought yogurt. Avoid yogurts containing modified food starch, gelatin, or gums since they prevent the yogurt from draining.

2 cups plain yogurt

Line fine-mesh strainer with 3 basket-style coffee filters or double layer of cheesecloth. Set prepared strainer over large measuring cup or bowl (there should be enough room for about 1 cup liquid to drain without touching strainer). Spoon yogurt into strainer, cover tightly with plastic wrap, and refrigerate until yogurt has released about 1 cup liquid and has creamy, cream cheese-like texture, at least 10 hours or up to 2 days. Transfer drained yogurt to clean container; discard liquid.

marinated artichokes

serves 6 to 8

This dish can be served cold or at room temperature.

2 lemons
1 cup chicken or vegetable broth
1 cup extra-virgin olive oil, divided
6 garlic cloves, peeled and smashed
¼ teaspoon red pepper flakes
2 sprigs fresh thyme
1 teaspoon table salt
¼ teaspoon pepper
3 pounds baby artichokes
   (2 to 4 ounces each)
2 tablespoons minced fresh mint

1 Using vegetable peeler, remove three 2-inch strips zest from 1 lemon. Grate ½ teaspoon zest from second lemon. Halve and juice lemons to yield ¼ cup juice; reserve spent halves.

2 Combine broth, ½ cup oil, garlic, pepper flakes, thyme sprigs, salt, pepper, and lemon zest strips in Instant Pot. Working with 1 artichoke at a time, cut top quarter off each and snap off dark outer leaves. Peel and trim stem, then cut artichoke in half lengthwise. Rub each artichoke half with spent lemon half and place in pot. Lock lid in place and close pressure release valve. Select high pressure cook function and cook for 3 minutes.

3 Turn off Instant Pot and quick-release pressure. Carefully remove lid, allowing steam to escape away from you. Transfer artichoke mixture to large bowl and stir in remaining ½ cup oil, reserved grated lemon zest, and reserved lemon juice. Let cool to room temperature, about 30 minutes. Stir in mint and season with salt and pepper to taste. Serve. (Artichokes and oil can be refrigerated for up to 4 days.)

marinated cauliflower and chickpeas with lemon and smoked paprika

serves 6 to 8

This dish can be served cold or at room temperature.

¼ cup extra-virgin olive oil, divided
5 garlic cloves, peeled and smashed
1½ teaspoons smoked paprika
½ cup chicken or vegetable broth
2 tablespoons sherry vinegar
½ lemon, quartered and sliced thin
1½ teaspoons sugar
⅛ teaspoon saffron threads, crumbled
1 teaspoon table salt
¼ teaspoon pepper
½ head cauliflower (1 pound), cored and
   cut into 1½-inch florets
1 cup canned chickpeas, rinsed
1 tablespoon minced fresh parsley

1 Using highest sauté function, cook 2 tablespoons oil and garlic in Instant Pot until garlic is fragrant and light golden brown, about 3 minutes. Turn off Instant Pot, then stir in paprika and let sit until fragrant, about 30 seconds. Stir in broth, vinegar, lemon slices, sugar, saffron, salt, and pepper. Stir in cauliflower and chickpeas. Lock lid in place and close pressure release valve. Select high pressure cook function and set cook time for 0 minutes. Once Instant Pot has reached pressure, immediately turn off pot and quick-release pressure. Carefully remove lid, allowing steam to escape away from you.

2 Transfer cauliflower mixture to large bowl and stir in remaining 2 tablespoons oil. Let cool to room temperature, about 30 minutes. Stir in parsley and season with salt and pepper to taste. Serve. (Cauliflower mixture can be refrigerated for up to 3 days.)

classic basil pesto

makes about 1½ cups

This Italian favorite is subject to endless riffing, but we stick to the basics here with floral basil, toasted pine nuts, and fruity olive oil.

- 6 garlic cloves, unpeeled
- ½ cup pine nuts
- 4 cups fresh basil leaves
- ¼ cup fresh parsley leaves
- 1 cup extra-virgin olive oil
- 1 ounce Parmesan cheese, grated fine (½ cup)

1 Toast garlic in 8-inch skillet over medium heat, shaking skillet occasionally, until softened and spotty brown, about 8 minutes. When garlic is cool enough to handle, remove and discard skins and chop coarsely. Meanwhile, toast pine nuts in now-empty skillet over medium heat, stirring often, until golden and fragrant, 4 to 5 minutes.

2 Place basil and parsley in 1-gallon zipper-lock bag. Pound bag with flat side of meat pounder or with rolling pin until all leaves are bruised.

3 Process garlic, pine nuts, and herbs in food processor until finely chopped, about 1 minute, scraping down sides of bowl as needed. With processor running, slowly add oil until incorporated. Transfer pesto to bowl, stir in Parmesan, and season with salt and pepper to taste. (Pesto can be refrigerated for up to 3 days or frozen for up to 3 months. To prevent browning, press plastic wrap flush to surface or top with thin layer of olive oil. Bring to room temperature before using.)

salsa verde
makes about 1½ cups
This all-purpose Spanish-style green sauce brings bright acidity to everything it touches.

- 4 cups fresh parsley leaves
- 8 garlic cloves, minced
- ¼ teaspoon table salt
- ¼ cup sherry vinegar
- 1 cup extra-virgin olive oil

Pulse parsley, garlic, and salt in food processor until parsley is coarsely chopped, about 10 pulses. Add vinegar and pulse briefly to combine. Transfer mixture to medium bowl and slowly whisk in oil until incorporated. Cover and let sit at room temperature for at least 30 minutes to allow flavors to meld. (Sauce can be refrigerated for up to 2 days; bring to room temperature before serving.)

chermoula
makes about 1½ cups
Chermoula is a Moroccan dressing made with a hefty amount of cilantro, and with cumin and paprika for roundness.

- 2¼ cups fresh cilantro leaves
- 8 garlic cloves, minced
- 1½ teaspoons ground cumin
- 1½ teaspoons paprika
- ½ teaspoon cayenne pepper
- ½ teaspoon table salt
- 6 tablespoons lemon juice (2 lemons)
- ¾ cup extra-virgin olive oil

Pulse cilantro, garlic, cumin, paprika, cayenne, and salt in food processor until cilantro is coarsely chopped, about 10 pulses. Add lemon juice and pulse briefly to combine. Transfer mixture to medium bowl and slowly whisk in oil until incorporated and mixture is emulsified. Cover and let sit at room temperature for at least 30 minutes to allow flavors to meld. (Sauce can be refrigerated for up to 2 days; bring to room temperature before serving.)

harissa
makes about 1 cup
Harissa is a potently spiced North African condiment. If you can't find Aleppo pepper, you can substitute 1½ teaspoons paprika and 1½ teaspoons finely chopped red pepper flakes.

- ¾ cup extra-virgin olive oil
- 12 garlic cloves, minced
- ¼ cup paprika
- 2 tablespoons ground coriander
- 2 tablespoons ground dried Aleppo pepper
- 2 teaspoons ground cumin
- 1½ teaspoons caraway seeds
- 1 teaspoon table salt

Combine all ingredients in bowl and microwave until bubbling and very fragrant, about 1 minute, stirring halfway through microwaving; let cool to room temperature. (Harissa can be refrigerated for up to 4 days.)

tzatziki
makes about 1 cup
Made from yogurt and cucumber, tzatziki is a traditional Greek sauce perfect for adding a cooling element to a dish. Using Greek yogurt here is key; do not substitute regular plain yogurt or the sauce will be very watery.

- ½ cucumber, peeled, halved lengthwise, seeded, and shredded
- ¼ teaspoon table salt
- ½ cup plain whole Greek yogurt
- 1 tablespoon extra-virgin olive oil
- 1 tablespoon minced fresh mint and/or dill
- 1 small garlic clove, minced

Toss cucumber with salt in colander and let drain for 15 minutes. Whisk yogurt, oil, mint, and garlic together in bowl, then stir in cucumber. Cover and refrigerate for at least 30 minutes to allow flavors to meld. Season with salt and pepper to taste. (Tzatziki can be refrigerated for up to 2 days.)

lemon-yogurt sauce

makes about 1 cup

Do not substitute low-fat or nonfat yogurt here.

- 1 cup plain whole-milk yogurt
- 1 teaspoon grated lemon zest plus 2 tablespoons juice
- 1 garlic clove, minced

Whisk all ingredients together in bowl and season with salt and pepper to taste. Cover and refrigerate for at least 30 minutes to allow flavors to meld. (Sauce can be refrigerated for up to 4 days.)

tahini sauce

makes about 1 cup

Our favorite brand of tahini is Ziyad.

- ½ cup tahini
- ½ cup water
- ¼ cup lemon juice (2 lemons)
- 2 garlic cloves, minced

Whisk all ingredients in bowl until smooth (mixture will appear broken at first). Season with salt and pepper to taste. Let sit at room temperature for at least 30 minutes to allow flavors to meld. (Sauce can be refrigerated for up to 4 days; bring to room temperature before serving.)

olive tapenade

makes about 1 cup

- ¾ cup pitted brine-cured green or black olives, chopped fine
- 1 small shallot, minced
- 2 tablespoons extra-virgin olive oil
- 1 tablespoon capers, rinsed and minced
- 1½ teaspoons red wine vinegar
- 1 teaspoon minced fresh oregano

Combine all ingredients in bowl. (Tapenade can be refrigerated for up to 1 week.)

finishing elements

quick pickled onions
makes about 1 cup

- 1 cup red wine vinegar
- ⅓ cup sugar
- ⅛ teaspoon table salt
- 1 red onion, halved and sliced thin through root end

Microwave vinegar, sugar, and salt in medium bowl until simmering, 1 to 2 minutes. Add onion and let sit, stirring occasionally, for 45 minutes. Drain onion and return to now-empty bowl. (Drained onions can be refrigerated for up to 1 week.)

quick preserved lemon
makes about 2 tablespoons
A floral, pungent, and elegant Moroccan staple.

- 8 (2-inch) strips lemon zest, minced, plus 2 teaspoons juice
- 1 teaspoon water
- ½ teaspoon sugar
- ½ teaspoon table salt

Combine all ingredients in bowl and microwave at 50 percent power until liquid evaporates, about 2 minutes, stirring and mashing lemon with back of spoon every 30 seconds; let cool to room temperature. (Lemon mixture can be refrigerated for up to 1 week.)

za'atar
makes about ½ cup
Earthy and citrusy, this irresistible spice mix can be sprinkled over anything that needs some oomph.

- ½ cup dried thyme, ground
- 2 tablespoons sesame seeds, toasted
- 1½ tablespoons ground sumac

Combine all ingredients in bowl. (Spice mix can be stored at room temperature in airtight container for up to 1 year.)

dukkah
makes about ½ cup
This eastern Mediterranean blend of nuts, seeds, and spices makes for a fragrant and crunchy garnish.

- 1½ teaspoons coriander seeds, toasted
- ¾ teaspoon cumin seeds, toasted
- ½ teaspoon fennel seeds, toasted
- 2 tablespoons sesame seeds, toasted
- 3 tablespoons shelled pistachios, toasted and chopped fine
- ½ teaspoon flake sea salt, such as Maldon
- ½ teaspoon pepper

Process coriander seeds, cumin seeds, and fennel seeds in spice grinder until finely ground, about 30 seconds. Add sesame seeds and pulse until coarsely ground, about 4 pulses; transfer to small bowl. Stir in pistachios, salt, and pepper. (Dukkah can be refrigerated for up to 3 months.)

garlic toasts
makes 8 slices
Be sure to use a high-quality crusty bread, such as a baguette; do not use sliced sandwich bread.

- 8 (1-inch-thick) slices rustic bread
- 1 large garlic clove, peeled
- 3 tablespoons extra-virgin olive oil

Adjust oven rack 6 inches from broiler element and heat broiler. Spread bread in single layer on rimmed baking sheet and broil, flipping as needed, until well toasted on both sides, about 4 minutes. Briefly rub 1 side of each toast with garlic, drizzle with oil, and season with salt and pepper to taste. Serve.

soups and stews

provençal chicken soup

serves 6 to 8   **total time** 1 hour 20 minutes

---

1 tablespoon extra-virgin olive oil

2 fennel bulbs, 2 tablespoons fronds minced, stalks discarded, bulbs halved, cored, and cut into ½-inch pieces

1 onion, chopped

1¾ teaspoons table salt

2 tablespoons tomato paste

4 garlic cloves, minced

1 tablespoon minced fresh thyme or 1 teaspoon dried

2 anchovy fillets, minced

7 cups water, divided

1 (14.5-ounce) can diced tomatoes, drained

2 carrots, peeled, halved lengthwise, and sliced ½ inch thick

2 (12-ounce) bone-in split chicken breasts, trimmed

4 (5- to 7-ounce) bone-in chicken thighs, trimmed

½ cup pitted brine-cured green olives, chopped

1 teaspoon grated orange zest

why this recipe works The fresh and fragrant herb and citrus flavors of Provence were our inspiration for this Mediterranean take on classic chicken soup. The Instant Pot made quick work of creating a substantial broth by extracting body-building gelatin from convenient bone-in, skin-on chicken parts. Just 20 minutes under pressure were enough to ensure the meat was moist and tender. We shredded the chicken (discarding the now-flavorless bones and skin) and added it back to the pot, along with some green olives, minced fennel fronds, and a teaspoon of orange zest to brighten the soup up. The anchovies boosted the savoriness of the soup without making it taste fishy. You can substitute 1½ teaspoons anchovy paste, if desired. If your fennel bulbs do not have fronds, you can substitute parsley or dill.

1 Using highest sauté function, heat oil in Instant Pot until shimmering. Add fennel pieces, onion, and salt and cook until vegetables are softened, about 5 minutes. Stir in tomato paste, garlic, thyme, and anchovies and cook until fragrant, about 30 seconds. Stir in 5 cups water, scraping up any browned bits, then stir in tomatoes and carrots. Nestle chicken breasts and thighs in pot.

2 Lock lid in place and close pressure release valve. Select high pressure cook function and cook for 20 minutes. Turn off Instant Pot and quick-release pressure. Carefully remove lid, allowing steam to escape away from you.

3 Transfer chicken to cutting board, let cool slightly, then shred into bite-size pieces using 2 forks; discard skin and bones.

4 Using wide, shallow spoon, skim excess fat from surface of soup. Stir chicken and any accumulated juices, olives, and remaining 2 cups water into soup and let sit until heated through, about 3 minutes. Stir in fennel fronds and orange zest, and season with salt and pepper to taste. Serve.

per serving
Cal 170; Total Fat 5g; Sat Fat 1g; Chol 60mg; Sodium 870mg; Total Carbs 11g, Fiber 3g, Total Sugar 5g; Added Sugar 0g; Protein 19g

spiced chicken soup with squash and chickpeas

serves 6 to 8   **total time** 1 hour 20 minutes

2 tablespoons extra-virgin olive oil

1 onion, chopped

1¾ teaspoons table salt

2 tablespoons tomato paste

4 garlic cloves, minced

1 tablespoon ground coriander

1½ teaspoons ground cumin

1 teaspoon ground cardamom

½ teaspoon ground allspice

¼ teaspoon cayenne pepper

7 cups water, divided

2 (12-ounce) bone-in split chicken breasts, trimmed

4 (5- to 7-ounce) bone-in chicken thighs, trimmed

1½ pounds butternut squash, peeled, seeded, and cut into 1½-inch pieces (4 cups)

1 (15-ounce) can chickpeas, rinsed

½ cup chopped fresh cilantro

why this recipe works We loved the ease and rich chicken flavor of our Provençal Chicken Soup (page 23) so much that we decided to use the same technique to create a warmly spiced version. Inspired by *hararat,* a North African blend of spices like cumin, coriander, and allspice (also called Libyan five-spice blend, or *bzaar*), we employed a blend of earthy spices with subtle heat. Hearty butternut cooked to silky perfection with the chicken under high pressure, and the canned chickpeas were simply warmed through, along with the shredded chicken, in the finished soup. Chopped cilantro added a final dose of herbal freshness.

1   Using highest sauté function, heat oil in Instant Pot until shimmering. Add onion and salt and cook until onion is softened, about 5 minutes. Stir in tomato paste, garlic, coriander, cumin, cardamom, allspice, and cayenne and cook until fragrant, about 30 seconds. Stir in 5 cups water, scraping up any browned bits. Nestle chicken breasts and thighs in pot, then arrange squash evenly around chicken.

2   Lock lid in place and close pressure release valve. Select high pressure cook function and cook for 20 minutes. Turn off Instant Pot and quick-release pressure. Carefully remove lid, allowing steam to escape away from you.

3   Transfer chicken to cutting board, let cool slightly, then shred into bite-size pieces using 2 forks; discard skin and bones.

4   Using wide, shallow spoon, skim excess fat from surface of soup, then break squash into bite-size pieces. Stir chicken and any accumulated juices, chickpeas, and remaining 2 cups water into soup and let sit until heated through, about 3 minutes. Stir in cilantro and season with salt and pepper to taste. Serve.

per serving
Cal 190; Total Fat 7g; Sat Fat 1g; Chol 60mg; Sodium 700mg; Total Carbs 16g, Fiber 4g, Total Sugar 3g; Added Sugar 0g; Protein 20g

spanish-style turkey meatball soup

serves 6 to 8   **total time** 1 hour

- 1 slice hearty white sandwich bread, torn into quarters
- ¼ cup whole milk
- 1 ounce Manchego cheese, grated (½ cup), plus extra for serving
- 5 tablespoons minced fresh parsley, divided
- ½ teaspoon table salt
- 1 pound ground turkey
- 1 tablespoon extra-virgin olive oil
- 1 onion, chopped
- 1 red bell pepper, stemmed, seeded, and cut into ¾-inch pieces
- 4 garlic cloves, minced
- 2 teaspoons smoked paprika
- ½ cup dry white wine
- 8 cups chicken broth
- 8 ounces kale, stemmed and chopped

why this recipe works This Spanish-style meatball soup boasts a sunset-colored broth and lean turkey meatballs kept moist and tender thanks to a panade (a paste made from bread and milk) and Manchego (a sharp Spanish sheep's-milk cheese). For our broth, we started with a *sofrito*, a traditional Spanish base of onion, bell pepper, and garlic, then added smoked paprika. After deglazing the pot with white wine, we poured in chicken broth, then carefully dropped in the meatballs and some chopped fresh kale. The soup required a mere 3 minutes under pressure, after which we brightened it with a sprinkling of minced parsley and a touch of extra Manchego. Be sure to use ground turkey, not ground turkey breast (also labeled 99 percent fat-free), in this recipe.

1 Using fork, mash bread and milk together into paste in large bowl. Stir in Manchego, 3 tablespoons parsley, and salt until combined. Add turkey and knead mixture with your hands until well combined. Pinch off and roll 2-teaspoon-size pieces of mixture into balls and arrange on large plate (you should have about 35 meatballs); set aside.

2 Using highest sauté function, heat oil in Instant Pot until shimmering. Add onion and bell pepper and cook until softened and lightly browned, 5 to 7 minutes. Stir in garlic and paprika and cook until fragrant, about 30 seconds. Stir in wine, scraping up any browned bits, and cook until almost completely evaporated, about 5 minutes. Stir in broth and kale, then gently submerge meatballs.

3 Lock lid in place and close pressure release valve. Select high pressure cook function and cook for 3 minutes. Turn off Instant Pot and quick-release pressure. Carefully remove lid, allowing steam to escape away from you.

4 Stir in remaining 2 tablespoons parsley and season with salt and pepper to taste. Serve, passing extra Manchego separately.

per serving
Cal 170; Total Fat 4.5g; Sat Fat 2.5g; Chol 25mg; Sodium 750mg; Total Carbs 9g, Fiber 2g, Total Sugar 4g; Added Sugar 0g; Protein 21g

beef oxtail soup with white beans, tomatoes, and aleppo pepper

serves 6 to 8   **total time** 2 hours

- 4 pounds oxtails, trimmed
- 1 teaspoon table salt
- 1 tablespoon extra-virgin olive oil
- 1 onion, chopped fine
- 2 carrots, peeled and chopped fine
- ¼ cup ground dried Aleppo pepper
- 6 garlic cloves, minced
- 2 tablespoons tomato paste
- ¾ teaspoon dried oregano
- ½ teaspoon ground cinnamon
- ½ teaspoon ground cumin
- 6 cups water
- 1 (28-ounce) can diced tomatoes, drained
- 1 (15-ounce) can navy beans, rinsed
- 1 tablespoon sherry vinegar
- ¼ cup chopped fresh parsley
- ½ preserved lemon, pulp and white pith removed, rind rinsed and minced (2 tablespoons)

why this recipe works Oxtails are widely underutilized, so we gave them star status in our take on the Turkish dish *etli kuru fasulye*, or "white beans with meat." The oxtails became moist and tender thanks to the Instant Pot's ability to draw out their plentiful collagen. Adding an eclectic mix of eastern Mediterranean ingredients gave the cooking liquid its character: sweet diced tomatoes, ground dried Aleppo pepper, and pungent oregano, along with warm cinnamon and cumin. After cooking, we added canned navy beans and sherry vinegar to create a hearty soup base, and sprinkled with preserved lemon, for an intense but subtly sweet citrusy finish. Try to buy oxtails that are approximately 2 inches thick and 2 to 4 inches in diameter. If using frozen oxtails, be sure to thaw them completely before using. If you can't find Aleppo pepper, you can substitute 1 tablespoon paprika and 2 teaspoons finely chopped red pepper flakes. If you can't find preserved lemons, you can substitute lemon zest or use our Quick Preserved Lemon (page 19).

1   Pat oxtails dry with paper towels and sprinkle with salt. Using highest sauté function, heat oil in Instant Pot for 5 minutes (or until just smoking). Brown half of oxtails, 4 to 6 minutes per side; transfer to plate. Set aside remaining uncooked oxtails.

2   Add onion and carrots to fat left in pot and cook, using highest sauté function, until softened, about 5 minutes. Stir in Aleppo pepper, garlic, tomato paste, oregano, cinnamon, and cumin and cook until fragrant, about 30 seconds. Stir in water, scraping up any browned bits, then stir in tomatoes. Nestle remaining uncooked oxtails into pot along with browned oxtails and add any accumulated juices.

3   Lock lid in place and close pressure release valve. Select high pressure cook function and cook for 45 minutes. Turn off Instant Pot and quick-release pressure. Carefully remove lid, allowing steam to escape away from you.

4 Transfer oxtails to cutting board, let cool slightly, then shred into bite-size pieces using 2 forks; discard bones and excess fat. Strain broth through fine-mesh strainer into large container; return solids to now-empty pot. Using wide, shallow spoon, skim excess fat from surface of liquid; return to pot.

5 Stir shredded oxtails and any accumulated juices and beans into pot. Using highest sauté function, cook until soup is heated through, about 5 minutes. Stir in vinegar and parsley and season with salt and pepper to taste. Serve, passing preserved lemon separately.

per serving
Cal 380; Total Fat 18g; Sat Fat 7g; Chol 130mg; Sodium 890mg; Total Carbs 17g, Fiber 5g, Total Sugar 4g; Added Sugar 0g; Protein 38g

spicy moroccan lamb and lentil soup

serves 6 to 8   **total time** 1 hour

- 1 pound lamb shoulder chops (blade or round bone), 1 to 1½ inches thick, trimmed and halved

- ¾ teaspoon table salt, divided

- ⅛ teaspoon pepper

- 1 tablespoon extra-virgin olive oil

- 1 onion, chopped fine

- ¼ cup harissa, plus extra for serving

- 1 tablespoon all-purpose flour

- 8 cups chicken broth

- 1 cup French green lentils, picked over and rinsed

- 1 (15-ounce) can chickpeas, rinsed

- 2 tomatoes, cored and cut into ¼-inch pieces

- ½ cup chopped fresh cilantro

why this recipe works *Harira* is an intense Moroccan soup of lentils, tomatoes, chickpeas, and meat (often chicken or lamb), and is best known as a dish with which to break the fast during the holy month of Ramadan. For our simplified recipe, we looked to our pantry for accessible, impactful flavor builders and chose harissa—a superspicy paste of hot chiles, spices, garlic, and olive oil. We browned lamb shoulder chops as our meat, then bloomed the aromatics in the rendered fat to achieve a sweet and smoky base. The Instant Pot ensured the lamb and lentils finished cooking at the same rate under pressure, and once the lamb was done, we shredded it and stirred it back into the pot along with canned chickpeas. Fresh tomatoes added just the right amount of sweetness and acidity, while a sprinkle of cilantro provided a bright, fresh finish. We prefer French green lentils, or *lentilles du Puy*, for this recipe, but it will work with any type of lentil except red or yellow. We like to use our homemade Harissa (page 17), but you can substitute store-bought harissa, though spiciness can vary greatly. Serve with yogurt, if desired.

1   Pat lamb dry with paper towels and sprinkle with ¼ teaspoon salt and pepper. Using highest sauté function, heat oil in Instant Pot for 5 minutes (or until just smoking). Place lamb in pot and cook until well browned on first side, about 4 minutes; transfer to plate.

2   Add onion and remaining ½ teaspoon salt to fat left in pot and cook, using highest sauté function, until softened, about 5 minutes. Stir in harissa and flour and cook until fragrant, about 30 seconds. Slowly whisk in broth, scraping up any browned bits and smoothing out any lumps. Stir in lentils, then nestle lamb into multicooker and add any accumulated juices.

3 Lock lid in place and close pressure release valve. Select high pressure cook function and cook for 10 minutes. Turn off Instant Pot and quick-release pressure. Carefully remove lid, allowing steam to escape away from you.

4 Transfer lamb to cutting board, let cool slightly, then shred into bite-size pieces using 2 forks; discard excess fat and bones. Stir lamb and chickpeas into soup and let sit until heated through, about 3 minutes. Season with salt and pepper to taste. Top individual portions with tomatoes and sprinkle with cilantro. Serve, passing extra harissa separately.

per serving
Cal 300; Total Fat 13g; Sat Fat 3g; Chol 35mg; Sodium 940mg; Total Carbs 24g, Fiber 6g, Total Sugar 4g; Added Sugar 0g; Protein 22g

beef stew with eggplant and potatoes

serves 6 to 8   **total time** 2 hours

- 2 pounds boneless short ribs, trimmed and cut into 1-inch pieces
- 1½ teaspoons table salt, divided
- 2 tablespoons extra-virgin olive oil
- 1 onion, chopped fine
- 3 tablespoons tomato paste
- ¼ cup all-purpose flour
- 3 garlic cloves, minced
- 1 tablespoon ground cumin
- 1 teaspoon ground turmeric
- 1 teaspoon ground cardamom
- ¾ teaspoon ground cinnamon
- 4 cups chicken broth
- 1 cup water
- 1 pound eggplant, cut into 1-inch pieces
- 1 pound Yukon Gold potatoes, unpeeled, cut into 1-inch pieces
- ½ cup chopped fresh mint or parsley

why this recipe works For this understated yet company-worthy Persian-inspired stew, we chose boneless short ribs for their fall-apart tender texture, and browned just half of them in our Instant Pot to achieve great savory depth. Onion, tomato paste, and garlic provided an aromatic backbone, while cumin, turmeric, cardamom, and cinnamon added warmth and complexity. Cubed Yukon Golds made for a heartier stew, and slightly broke down during cooking to yield a velvety textured base. While eggplant often needs pre-treatment such as salting to ensure a dense and tender consistency, we found we could skip this time-consuming step and simply stir unpeeled pieces in with the potatoes. Cutting the eggplant into 1-inch pieces ensured it didn't fall apart during cooking. A sprinkling of fresh mint completed the dish.

1 Pat beef dry with paper towels and sprinkle with 1 teaspoon salt. Using highest sauté function, heat oil in Instant Pot for 5 minutes (or until just smoking). Brown half of beef on all sides, 7 to 9 minutes; transfer to bowl. Set aside remaining uncooked beef.

2 Add onion to fat left in pot and cook, using highest sauté function, until softened, about 5 minutes. Stir in tomato paste, flour, garlic, cumin, turmeric, cardamom, cinnamon, and remaining ½ teaspoon salt. Cook until fragrant, about 1 minute. Slowly whisk in broth and water, scraping up any browned bits. Stir in eggplant and potatoes. Nestle remaining uncooked beef into pot along with browned beef, and add any accumulated juices.

3 Lock lid in place and close pressure release valve. Select high pressure cook function and cook for 30 minutes. Turn off Instant Pot and quick-release pressure. Carefully remove lid, allowing steam to escape away from you.

4 Using wide, shallow spoon, skim excess fat from surface of stew. Stir in mint and season with salt and pepper to taste. Serve.

per serving
Cal 330; Total Fat 15g; Sat Fat 5g; Chol 65mg; Sodium 790mg; Total Carbs 22g, Fiber 4g, Total Sugar 4g; Added Sugar 0g; Protein 26g

sicilian fish stew

serves 4 to 6   **total time** 45 minutes

---

2 tablespoons extra-virgin olive oil

2 onions, chopped fine

1 teaspoon table salt

½ teaspoon pepper

1 teaspoon minced fresh thyme or ¼ teaspoon dried

Pinch red pepper flakes

4 garlic cloves, minced, divided

1 (28-ounce) can whole peeled tomatoes, drained with juice reserved, chopped coarse

1 (8-ounce) bottle clam juice

¼ cup dry white wine

¼ cup golden raisins

2 tablespoons capers, rinsed

1½ pounds skinless swordfish steak, 1 to 1½ inches thick, cut into 1-inch pieces

¼ cup pine nuts, toasted

¼ cup minced fresh mint

1 teaspoon grated orange zest

why this recipe works Many Sicilian dishes exhibit the strong influence of Arabic cooking through the use of dried fruits and nuts, including tomato-based fish stew, which, with its balance of sweet, sour, and salty notes, is common in the region. We chose swordfish because its meaty texture and distinct flavor could stand up to a symphony of bold flavors. For the base, we created a quick stock using aromatic onions, garlic, thyme, and red pepper flakes simmered with white wine, whole peeled tomatoes, and clam juice, and mixed in golden raisins and capers for sweet and briny bursts of flavor. After just 1 minute under pressure, the swordfish emerged tender and succulent. To finish our stew, we put together a twist on gremolata, a classic Italian herb condiment usually made with lemon zest and parsley. Here, we swapped those elements for orange zest and mint, and stirred in toasted pine nuts for added crunch. Halibut is a good substitute for the swordfish. Serve with crusty bread to dip into the broth.

1 Using highest sauté function, heat oil in Instant Pot until shimmering. Add onions, salt, and pepper and cook until onions are softened, about 5 minutes. Stir in thyme, pepper flakes, and three-quarters of garlic and cook until fragrant, about 30 seconds. Stir in tomatoes and reserved juice, clam juice, wine, raisins, and capers. Nestle swordfish into pot and spoon some cooking liquid over top.

2 Lock lid in place and close pressure release valve. Select high pressure cook function and cook for 1 minute. Turn off Instant Pot and quick-release pressure. Carefully remove lid, allowing steam to escape away from you.

3 Combine pine nuts, mint, orange zest, and remaining garlic in bowl. Season stew with salt and pepper to taste. Sprinkle individual portions with pine nut mixture before serving.

per serving
Cal 320; Total Fat 16g; Sat Fat 3g; Chol 75mg; Sodium 920mg; Total Carbs 16g, Fiber 3g, Total Sugar 10g; Added Sugar 0g; Protein 25g

creamy carrot soup with warm spices

serves 6 to 8   **total time** 1 hour

- 2 tablespoons extra-virgin olive oil
- 2 onions, chopped
- 1 teaspoon table salt
- 1 tablespoon grated fresh ginger
- 1 tablespoon ground coriander
- 1 tablespoon ground fennel
- 1 teaspoon ground cinnamon
- 4 cups vegetable or chicken broth
- 2 cups water
- 2 pounds carrots, peeled and cut into 2-inch pieces
- ½ teaspoon baking soda
- 2 tablespoons pomegranate molasses
- ½ cup plain Greek yogurt
- ½ cup hazelnuts, toasted, skinned, and chopped
- ½ cup chopped fresh cilantro or mint

why this recipe works Pantry-friendly carrots and onions plus a few delicately balanced aromatics cook for a mere 3 minutes under pressure in the Instant Pot to produce this simple but luxurious soup. In many popular carrot soup recipes, the clean brightness of carrots is muted by the addition of other vegetables or fruits or dairy, so we kept these extras to a minimum. Taking a cue from the eastern Mediterranean, we added a combination of fresh ginger plus ground coriander, fennel, and cinnamon. A touch of baking soda helped break down the carrots, and after a quick spin in the blender we had a satiny-smooth and creamy soup without adding cream. To finish, we topped individual portions with a bit of tart Greek yogurt, a drizzle of pomegranate molasses to underscore the natural sweetness of the carrots, some toasted hazelnuts, and fresh herbs.

1 Using highest sauté function, heat oil in Instant Pot until shimmering. Add onions and salt and cook until onions are softened, about 5 minutes. Stir in ginger, coriander, fennel, and cinnamon and cook until fragrant, about 30 seconds. Stir in broth, water, carrots, and baking soda.

2 Lock lid in place and close pressure release valve. Select high pressure cook function and cook for 3 minutes. Turn off Instant Pot and quick-release pressure. Carefully remove lid, allowing steam to escape away from you.

3 Working in batches, process soup in blender until smooth, 1 to 2 minutes. Return processed soup to Instant Pot and bring to simmer using highest sauté function. Season with salt and pepper to taste. Drizzle individual portions with pomegranate molasses and top with yogurt, hazelnuts, and cilantro before serving.

per serving
Cal 190; Total Fat 11g; Sat Fat 2.5g; Chol 5mg; Sodium 820mg; Total Carbs 20g, Fiber 5g, Total Sugar 10g; Added Sugar 0g; Protein 4g

vegetable and chickpea stew

serves 6 to 8   **total time** 1 hour

¼ cup extra-virgin olive oil, plus extra for drizzling

2 red bell peppers, stemmed, seeded, and cut into 1-inch pieces

1 onion, chopped fine

½ teaspoon table salt

½ teaspoon pepper

1½ tablespoons baharat

4 garlic cloves, minced

1 tablespoon tomato paste

4 cups vegetable or chicken broth

1 (28-ounce) can whole peeled tomatoes, drained with juice reserved, chopped

1 pound Yukon Gold potatoes, peeled and cut into ½-inch pieces

2 zucchini, quartered lengthwise and sliced 1 inch thick

1 (15-ounce) can chickpeas, rinsed

⅓ cup chopped fresh mint

why this recipe works Bold spices are an exciting contrast to the bounty of vegetables in this Lebanese-inspired stew. We wanted to cut down on the lengthy list of spices included in many Lebanese recipes, so we turned to *baharat*, a potent Middle Eastern spice blend. Using the sauté function, we started by browning the bell peppers and onion to develop depth. The baharat was next, followed by a little garlic and tomato paste. After cooking it all under pressure, we simmered the delicate zucchini in the stew to ensure that it remained green and tender, adding convenient canned chickpeas to warm through. A little olive oil drizzled at the end provided richness, while chopped mint added freshness. If you can't find baharat, you can substitute 1½ teaspoons ground nutmeg, 1½ teaspoons paprika, ½ teaspoon ground coriander, ½ teaspoon ground cinnamon, and ½ teaspoon ground cumin.

1   Using highest sauté function, heat oil in Instant Pot until shimmering. Add bell pepper, onion, salt, and pepper and cook until vegetables are softened and lightly browned, 5 to 7 minutes. Stir in baharat, garlic, and tomato paste and cook until fragrant, about 1 minute. Stir in broth and tomatoes and reserved juice, scraping up any browned bits, then stir in potatoes.

2   Lock lid in place and close pressure release valve. Select high pressure cook function and cook for 9 minutes. Turn off Instant Pot and quick-release pressure. Carefully remove lid, allowing steam to escape away from you.

3   Stir zucchini and chickpeas into stew and cook, using highest sauté function, until zucchini is tender, 10 to 15 minutes. Turn off multicooker. Season with salt and pepper to taste. Drizzle individual portions with extra oil, and sprinkle with mint before serving.

per serving
Cal 200; Total Fat 8g; Sat Fat 1g; Chol 0mg; Sodium 740mg; Total Carbs 28g, Fiber 5g, Total Sugar 7g; Added Sugar 0g; Protein 5g

farro and leek soup

serves 6 to 8   **total time** 1 hour

1 cup whole farro

1 tablespoon extra-virgin olive oil, plus extra for drizzling

3 ounces pancetta, chopped fine

1 pound leeks, ends trimmed, chopped, and washed thoroughly

2 carrots, peeled and chopped

1 celery rib, chopped

8 cups chicken broth, plus extra as needed

½ cup minced fresh parsley

Grated Parmesan cheese

why this recipe works Farro is a staple of Umbria, in central Italy, where it predates common wheat. We were intrigued by classic *minestra di farro*, a hearty soup in which farro's nuttiness shines. Coarsely ground farro is the traditional choice, but since whole farro is easier to find stateside, we were happy to discover that it's a cinch to grind your own; six pulses in a blender cracked a portion of the grains, freeing just enough starch to give our soup rich body. We used readily accessible pancetta to deliver a meaty boost. A full pound of leeks gave this soup a uniquely pungent sweetness (rounded out by carrots and celery), and we loved that our Instant Pot softened even the dark green parts of the leeks in the short time it took the farro to cook through. A sprinkling of parsley and some freshly grated Parmesan finished this humble soup. Do not use quick-cooking, presteamed, or pearled farro (read the ingredient list on the package to determine this) in this recipe. Bacon can be used in place of the pancetta.

1   Pulse farro in blender until about half of grains are broken into smaller pieces, about 6 pulses; set aside.

2   Using highest sauté function, heat oil in Instant Pot until shimmering. Add pancetta and cook until lightly browned, 3 to 5 minutes. Stir in leeks, carrots, and celery and cook until softened, about 5 minutes. Stir in broth, scraping up any browned bits, then stir in farro.

3   Lock lid in place and close pressure release valve. Select high pressure cook function and cook for 8 minutes. Turn off Instant Pot and quick-release pressure. Carefully remove lid, allowing steam to escape away from you.

4   Adjust consistency with extra hot broth as needed. Stir in parsley and season with salt and pepper to taste. Drizzle individual portions with extra oil and top with Parmesan before serving.

per serving
Cal 180; Total Fat 6g; Sat Fat 1.5g; Chol 10mg; Sodium 950mg; Total Carbs 25g, Fiber 1g, Total Sugar 4g; Added Sugar 0g; Protein 7g

lentil and chorizo soup

serves 6 to 8   **total time** 1 hour

1 tablespoon extra-virgin olive oil, plus extra for drizzling

8 ounces Spanish-style chorizo sausage, quartered lengthwise and sliced thin

4 garlic cloves, minced

1½ teaspoons smoked paprika

5 cups water

1 pound (2¼ cups) French green lentils, picked over and rinsed

4 cups chicken broth

1 tablespoon sherry vinegar, plus extra for seasoning

2 bay leaves

1 teaspoon table salt

1 large onion, peeled

2 carrots, peeled and halved crosswise

½ cup slivered almonds, toasted

½ cup minced fresh parsley

why this recipe works The combination of earthy lentils and smoked paprika–scented chorizo sausage is enjoyed throughout Spain with varying degrees of brothiness. We wanted to create a soup that featured whole lentils suspended in a creamy, but not too thick, broth. Tasters agreed that 8 ounces of chorizo was the perfect amount to render just enough meaty flavor and richness into the soup. To save prep time, we cooked our vegetables whole with the lentils under pressure, pureed them quickly in the food processor, then returned them to the soup to achieve a velvety broth. We prefer French green lentils, or *lentilles du Puy*, for this recipe, but it will work with any type of lentil except red or yellow. If Spanish-style chorizo is not available, Portuguese linguiça or Polish kielbasa can be substituted. Red wine vinegar can be substituted for the sherry vinegar.

1 Using highest sauté function, heat oil in Instant Pot until shimmering. Add chorizo and cook until lightly browned, 3 to 5 minutes. Stir in garlic and paprika and cook until fragrant, about 30 seconds. Stir in water, scraping up any browned bits, then stir in lentils, broth, vinegar, bay leaves, and salt. Nestle onion and carrots into pot.

2 Lock lid in place and close pressure release valve. Select high pressure cook function and cook for 14 minutes. Turn off Instant Pot and quick-release pressure. Carefully remove lid, allowing steam to escape away from you.

3 Discard bay leaves. Using slotted spoon, transfer onion and carrots to food processor and process until smooth, about 1 minute, scraping down sides of bowl as needed. Stir vegetable mixture into lentils and season with salt, pepper, and extra vinegar to taste. Drizzle individual portions with extra oil, and sprinkle with almonds and parsley before serving.

per serving
Cal 360; Total Fat 16g; Sat Fat 4.5g; Chol 25mg; Sodium 950mg; Total Carbs 30g, Fiber 7g, Total Sugar 5g; Added Sugar 0g; Protein 21g

tuscan white bean and escarole soup

serves 6 to 8   **total time** 1 hour 30 minutes, plus brining time

1½ tablespoons table salt, for brining

1 pound (2½ cups) dried cannellini beans, picked over and rinsed

1 large onion, chopped coarse

2 celery ribs, chopped coarse

4 garlic cloves, peeled

1 (28-ounce) can whole peeled tomatoes

2 tablespoons extra-virgin olive oil, plus extra for drizzling

1 fennel bulb, stalks discarded, bulb halved, cored, and cut into ½-inch pieces

½ teaspoon table salt

⅛ teaspoon red pepper flakes

8 cups chicken broth

1 small head escarole, trimmed and cut into ½-inch pieces (8 cups)

2 large egg yolks

½ cup chopped fresh parsley

1 tablespoon minced fresh oregano

Grated Pecorino Romano cheese

Lemon wedges

why this recipe works *Acquacotta*, a traditional Italian favorite, features cannellini beans, tender fennel, and subtly bitter escarole suspended in a satiny egg yolk–thickened broth. Brined dried cannellini beans have a beautifully soft texture when cooked, and the Instant Pot is a great way to cook them evenly. A food processor made quick work of finely chopping the celery, onion, and canned tomatoes that make up the broth. To keep the escarole fresh-tasting and slightly crunchy, we waited to add it until after releasing the pressure. Before adding the egg yolks, we first whisked them together with some reserved cooking liquid to avoid curdling, then we stirred the mixture into the broth along with parsley and aromatic oregano. Ladling the soup over Garlic Toasts (page 19) makes it an even heartier meal. If escarole is unavailable, you can substitute 8 ounces of kale. We prefer Pecorino Romano's salty flavor, but Parmesan can be substituted, if desired. See page 8 for more information on brining beans.

1 Dissolve 1½ tablespoons salt in 2 quarts cold water in large container. Add beans and soak at room temperature for at least 8 hours or up to 24 hours. Drain and rinse well.

2 Pulse onion, celery, and garlic in food processor until very finely chopped, 15 to 20 pulses, scraping down sides of bowl as needed; set aside. Add tomatoes and their juice to now-empty processor and pulse until tomatoes are finely chopped, 10 to 12 pulses; set aside.

3 Using highest sauté function, heat oil in Instant Pot until shimmering. Add onion mixture, fennel, ½ teaspoon salt, and pepper flakes and cook until fennel begins to soften, 7 to 9 minutes. Stir in broth, tomatoes, and beans.

4 Lock lid in place and close pressure release valve. Select high pressure cook function and cook for 1 minute. Turn off Instant Pot and let pressure release naturally for 15 minutes. Quick-release any remaining pressure, then carefully remove lid, allowing steam to escape away from you.

5 Measure out and reserve 1 cup hot broth. Stir escarole into multicooker, 1 handful at a time, and let cook in residual heat until escarole is wilted, about 5 minutes.

6 Gently whisk egg yolks together in small bowl. Whisking constantly, slowly add reserved broth to eggs until combined. Stir yolk mixture, parsley, and oregano into soup. Season with salt and pepper to taste. Top individual portions with Pecorino and drizzle with extra oil. Serve with lemon wedges.

per serving
Cal 300; Total Fat 6g; Sat Fat 1g; Chol 45mg; Sodium 1040mg; Total Carbs 45g, Fiber 23g, Total Sugar 6g; Added Sugar 0g; Protein 16g

gigante bean soup with celery and olives

serves 6 to 8 **total time** 1 hour, plus brining time

1½ tablespoons table salt, for brining

1 pound (2½ cups) dried gigante beans, picked over and rinsed

2 tablespoons extra-virgin olive oil, plus extra for drizzling

5 celery ribs, cut into ½-inch pieces, plus ½ cup leaves, minced

1 onion, chopped

½ teaspoon table salt

4 garlic cloves, minced

4 cups vegetable or chicken broth

4 cups water

2 bay leaves

½ cup pitted kalamata olives, chopped

2 tablespoons minced fresh marjoram or oregano

Lemon wedges

why this recipe works The mellow, vegetal broth of our Greek bean soup comes alive when individual portions are topped with a generous heaping of finely chopped tender and slightly sweet celery leaves, kalamata olives, and fragrant fresh marjoram. The floral mixture perfumes the soup and complements the pillowy-soft gigante beans. We soaked the beans overnight in salted water, which softened their skins and made them less prone to bursting. If you can't find gigante beans, you can substitute cannellini beans; reduce the time under pressure to 1 minute in step 3. If celery leaves are not available, substitute ¼ cup minced celery plus ¼ cup minced fresh parsley. See page 8 for more information on brining beans.

1   Dissolve 1½ tablespoons salt in 2 quarts cold water in large container. Add beans and soak at room temperature for at least 8 hours or up to 24 hours. Drain and rinse well.

2   Using highest sauté function, heat oil in Instant Pot until shimmering. Add celery pieces, onion, and ½ teaspoon salt and cook until vegetables are softened, about 5 minutes. Stir in garlic and cook until fragrant, about 30 seconds. Stir in broth, water, beans, and bay leaves.

3   Lock lid in place and close pressure release valve. Select high pressure cook function and cook for 6 minutes. Turn off Instant Pot and let pressure release naturally for 15 minutes. Quick-release any remaining pressure, then carefully remove lid, allowing steam to escape away from you.

4   Combine celery leaves, olives, and marjoram in bowl. Discard bay leaves. Season soup with salt and pepper to taste. Top individual portions with celery-olive mixture and drizzle with extra oil. Serve with lemon wedges.

per serving
Cal 250; Total Fat 4.5g; Sat Fat 0.5g; Chol 0mg; Sodium 660mg; Total Carbs 40g, Fiber 11g, Total Sugar 6g; Added Sugar 0g; Protein 13g

all-purpose chicken broth

makes 3 quarts   **total time** 2 hours 20 minutes

3 pounds chicken wings

1 tablespoon vegetable oil

1 onion, chopped

3 garlic cloves, lightly crushed and peeled

12 cups water, divided

½ teaspoon table salt

3 bay leaves

why this recipe works To maximize the chicken flavor in our broth, we tested many combinations of chicken parts and found chicken wings to be the surprise winner—the Instant Pot eked out every last bit of chickeny goodness and gelatin from the bones, resulting in a broth that was remarkably clear and that had a great silky texture. Browning the chicken wings was an easy way to deepen their flavor; we also browned some onion and garlic. A few bay leaves were the only other seasoning we needed to complement the broth.

1 Pat chicken wings dry with paper towels. Using highest sauté function, heat oil in Instant Pot for 5 minutes (or until just smoking). Brown half of chicken wings on all sides, about 10 minutes; transfer to bowl. Repeat with remaining chicken wings; transfer to bowl.

2 Add onion to fat left in pot and cook until softened and well browned, 8 to 10 minutes. Stir in garlic and cook until fragrant, about 30 seconds. Stir in 1 cup water, scraping up any browned bits. Stir in remaining 11 cups water, salt, bay leaves, and chicken and any accumulated juices.

3 Lock lid in place and close pressure release valve. Select high pressure cook function and cook for 1 hour. Turn off Instant Pot and let pressure release naturally for 15 minutes. Quick-release any remaining pressure, then carefully remove lid, allowing steam to escape away from you.

4 Strain broth through fine-mesh strainer into large container, pressing on solids to extract as much liquid as possible; discard solids. Using wide, shallow spoon, skim excess fat from surface of broth. (Broth can be refrigerated for up to 4 days or frozen for up to 2 months.)

per 1-cup serving
Cal 20; Total Fat 0g; Sat Fat 0g; Chol 0mg; Sodium 95mg; Total Carbs 0g, Fiber 0g, Total Sugar 0g; Added Sugar 0g; Protein 4g

all-purpose vegetable broth

makes 3 quarts   **total time** 2 hours 10 minutes

- 1 tablespoon vegetable oil
- 3 onions, chopped
- 4 scallions, chopped
- 2 carrots, peeled and chopped
- 2 celery ribs, chopped
- 15 garlic cloves, smashed and peeled
- 12 cups water, divided
- ½ head cauliflower (1 pound), cored and cut into 1-inch pieces
- 1 tomato, cored and chopped
- 8 sprigs fresh thyme
- 1 teaspoon peppercorns
- ½ teaspoon table salt
- 3 bay leaves

why this recipe works Vegetable broth is essential to vegetarian cooking, enhancing meat-free dishes with clean vegetal flavor. The moist heat of the Instant Pot easily heightens vegetables' subtleties, making for a full-flavored broth. A base of onions, scallions, carrots, and celery, along with a generous dose of garlic, provided a strong and balanced backbone, and the addition of half a head of cauliflower, cut into florets and added with the water, gave our broth pleasant earthiness and nuttiness. Finally, a single tomato added acidic balance, and thyme sprigs, peppercorns, and bay leaves rounded out the aromatic notes. Although we wanted to be able to dump all the vegetables into the cooker raw, we found that we needed the depth achieved from browning the aromatics with the sauté function. To avoid a cloudy broth, do not press on the solids when straining.

1   Using highest sauté function, heat oil in Instant Pot until shimmering. Add onions, scallions, carrots, celery, and garlic and cook until vegetables are softened and lightly browned, about 15 minutes. Stir in 1 cup water, scraping up any browned bits, then stir in remaining 11 cups water, cauliflower, tomato, thyme sprigs, peppercorns, salt, and bay leaves.

2   Lock lid in place and close pressure release valve. Select high pressure cook function and cook for 1 hour. Turn off Instant Pot and let pressure release naturally for 15 minutes. Quick-release any remaining pressure, then carefully remove lid, allowing steam to escape away from you.

3   Strain broth through fine-mesh strainer into large container, without pressing on solids; discard solids. (Broth can be refrigerated for up to 4 days or frozen for up to 2 months.)

per 1-cup serving
Cal 9; Total Fat 0g; Sat Fat 0g; Chol 0mg; Sodium 95mg; Total Carbs 0g, Fiber 0g, Total Sugar 0g; Added Sugar 0g; Protein 1g

grains, beans, and pasta

spiced rice pilaf with sweet potatoes and pomegranate

serves 4 to 6 **total time** 45 minutes

---

2 tablespoons extra-virgin olive oil

1 onion, chopped fine

½ teaspoon table salt

2 garlic cloves, minced

1½ teaspoons ground turmeric

1 teaspoon ground coriander

⅛ teaspoon cayenne pepper

2 cups chicken broth

1½ cups long-grain white rice, rinsed

12 ounces sweet potato, peeled, quartered lengthwise, and sliced ½ inch thick

½ preserved lemon, pulp and white pith removed, rind rinsed and minced (2 tablespoons)

½ cup shelled pistachios, toasted and chopped

¼ cup fresh cilantro leaves

¼ cup pomegranate seeds

why this recipe works The Instant Pot is a foolproof way to avoid mushy, blown-out rice and instead yield fluffy individual grains. This pilaf gets its vibrant color (and subtle spice) from a healthy dose of turmeric, coriander, and cayenne. We bloomed the spices right in the pot, then stirred in chicken broth, rice, and sweet potato. After just a few minutes under pressure, the firm sweet potato transformed into fudgy little chunks dispersed among perfectly cooked rice. For textural contrast, we deployed some finishing sprinkles—pomegranate seeds for bright little pops of color and sweetness, and savory, crunchy pistachios to counter the tender sweet potato. We think the fragrant and floral notes of preserved lemon are an important addition to this dish, but if you can't find it, you can substitute 1 tablespoon lemon zest or use our Quick Preserved Lemon (page 19).

1 Using highest sauté function, heat oil in Instant Pot until shimmering. Add onion and salt and cook until onion is softened, about 5 minutes. Stir in garlic, turmeric, coriander, and cayenne and cook until fragrant, about 30 seconds. Stir in broth, rice, and sweet potato.

2 Lock lid in place and close pressure release valve. Select high pressure cook function and cook for 4 minutes. Turn off Instant Pot and quick-release pressure. Carefully remove lid, allowing steam to escape away from you.

3 Add preserved lemon and gently fluff rice with fork to combine. Lay clean dish towel over pot, replace lid, and let sit for 5 minutes. Season with salt and pepper to taste. Transfer to serving dish and sprinkle with pistachios, cilantro, and pomegranate seeds. Serve.

per serving
Cal 320; Total Fat 10g; Sat Fat 1.5g; Chol 0mg; Sodium 500mg; Total Carbs 52g, Fiber 3g, Total Sugar 5g; Added Sugar 0g; Protein 8g

freekeh pilaf with dates and pistachios

serves 4 to 6   **total time** 30 minutes

---

2 tablespoons extra-virgin olive oil, plus extra for drizzling

1 shallot, minced

1½ teaspoons grated fresh ginger

½ teaspoon table salt

¼ teaspoon ground coriander

¼ teaspoon ground cumin

¼ teaspoon pepper

1¾ cups water

1½ cups cracked freekeh, rinsed

3 ounces pitted dates, chopped (½ cup)

¼ cup shelled pistachios, toasted and coarsely chopped

1½ tablespoons lemon juice

¼ cup chopped fresh mint

why this recipe works Freekeh, fire-roasted immature durum wheat, is a nutrient-packed grain often used in eastern Mediterranean and North African cooking. For a pilaf that accentuates freekeh's earthiness, we paired it with warm spices and refreshing mint. A quick sauté of the aromatics in the Instant Pot was sufficient to soften a shallot and bloom the spices, and then we just had to add the freekeh and water and cook under pressure. Studded with sweet dates and toasted pistachios, our pilaf was a hearty, healthful option for a unique side or satisfying lunch. You can find freekeh in the grain aisle or natural foods section of most well-stocked supermarkets; it is sometimes spelled *frikeh* or *farik*. Do not substitute whole freekeh, as it requires a different cooking method and will not work in this recipe.

1 Using highest sauté function, heat oil in Instant Pot until shimmering. Add shallot, ginger, salt, coriander, cumin, and pepper and cook until shallot is softened, about 2 minutes. Stir in water and freekeh.

2 Lock lid in place and close pressure release valve. Select high pressure cook function and cook for 4 minutes. Turn off Instant Pot and quick-release pressure. Carefully remove lid, allowing steam to escape away from you.

3 Add dates, pistachios, and lemon juice and gently fluff freekeh with fork to combine. Season with salt and pepper to taste. Transfer to serving dish, sprinkle with mint, and drizzle with extra oil. Serve.

per serving
Cal 280; Total Fat 8g; Sat Fat 1g; Chol 0mg; Sodium 200mg; Total Carbs 46g, Fiber 9g, Total Sugar 10g; Added Sugar 0g; Protein 8g

weeknight paella

serves 4 to 6   **total time** 1 hour

1 tablespoon extra-virgin olive oil

8 ounces Spanish-style chorizo sausage, sliced on bias ½ inch thick

1 onion, chopped fine

¼ teaspoon table salt

2 cups Arborio rice, picked over and rinsed

2 tablespoons tomato paste

6 garlic cloves, minced

1 teaspoon smoked paprika

¼ cup dry white wine

1 pound boneless, skinless chicken thighs, trimmed and quartered

2 cups chicken broth

2 cups water

¼ teaspoon saffron threads, crumbled

8 ounces large shrimp (26 to 30 per pound), peeled and deveined

½ cup frozen peas, thawed

2 tablespoons chopped fresh parsley

why this recipe works This saffron-scented rice dish from Valencia, Spain, is a showstopper, but unusual ingredients and complicated preparations can make it intimidating to tackle at home. We wanted chewy rice accompanied by low-prep, easy-to-find proteins—we chose smoky chorizo, succulent chicken, and juicy shrimp—minus the unwieldy two-handled paella pan and laundry list of ingredients. The Instant Pot ensured the Arborio rice (our choice for its firm, toothsome texture) and chicken thighs were ready in a snap (and simultaneously!), and once they were cooked we took advantage of the residual heat to cook our shrimp and peas gently. Tomato paste gave us concentrated tomatoey depth, and chicken broth, white wine, smoked paprika, and saffron provided the right amount of bold, balanced flavor. Dry-cured Spanish chorizo is the sausage of choice for paella, but fresh chorizo or linguiça sausage is an acceptable substitute. Do not substitute larger shrimp here; they will not cook through in time. Serve with lemon wedges.

1   Using highest sauté function, heat oil in Instant Pot until shimmering. Add chorizo, onion, and salt and cook until onion is softened, about 5 minutes. Add rice and cook, stirring occasionally, until edges begin to turn translucent, about 3 minutes. Stir in tomato paste, garlic, and paprika and cook until fragrant, about 30 seconds. Stir in wine, scraping up any browned bits, then stir in chicken, broth, water, and saffron.

2   Lock lid in place and close pressure release valve. Select high pressure cook function and cook for 1 minute. Turn off Instant Pot and quick-release pressure. Carefully remove lid, allowing steam to escape away from you.

3   Stir shrimp and peas into rice, cover, and let sit until shrimp are opaque throughout, 5 to 7 minutes. Season with salt and pepper to taste. Sprinkle with parsley and serve.

per serving
Cal 560; Total Fat 22g; Sat Fat 7g; Chol 140mg; Sodium 1010mg; Total Carbs 54g, Fiber 3g, Total Sugar 2g; Added Sugar 0g; Protein 36g

bulgur with chickpeas, spinach, and za'atar

serves 4 to 6   **total time** 45 minutes

3 tablespoons extra-virgin olive oil, divided

1 onion, chopped fine

½ teaspoon table salt

3 garlic cloves, minced

2 tablespoons za'atar, divided

1 cup medium-grind bulgur, rinsed

1 (15-ounce) can chickpeas, rinsed

1½ cups water

5 ounces (5 cups) baby spinach, chopped

1 tablespoon lemon juice, plus lemon wedges for serving

why this recipe works Hearty bulgur, creamy, nutty chickpeas, and fresh spinach come together in this side dish or light main, with a boost from the aromatic eastern Mediterranean spice blend za'atar, with its fragrant wild herbs, toasted sesame seeds, and tangy sumac. Fluffing the bulgur straight after cooking and then letting it sit was crucial to achieving perfectly cooked grains that weren't soggy: Agitating the grains and putting a towel under the lid allowed excess moisture in the pot to be absorbed. We used the residual heat from the bulgur to wilt baby spinach gently without turning it gummy. When shopping, don't confuse bulgur with cracked wheat, which has a much longer cooking time and will not work in this recipe. We like to use our homemade Za'atar (page 19), but you can substitute store-bought.

1   Using highest sauté function, heat 2 tablespoons oil in Instant Pot until shimmering. Add onion and salt and cook until onion is softened, about 5 minutes. Stir in garlic and 1 tablespoon za'atar and cook until fragrant, about 30 seconds. Stir in bulgur, chickpeas, and water.

2   Lock lid in place and close pressure release valve. Select high pressure cook function and cook for 1 minute. Turn off Instant Pot and quick-release pressure. Carefully remove lid, allowing steam to escape away from you.

3   Gently fluff bulgur with fork. Lay clean dish towel over pot, replace lid, and let sit for 5 minutes. Add spinach, lemon juice, remaining 1 tablespoon za'atar, and remaining 1 tablespoon oil and gently toss to combine. Season with salt and pepper to taste. Serve with lemon wedges.

per serving
Cal 200; Total Fat 8g; Sat Fat 1g; Chol 0mg; Sodium 320mg; Total Carbs 28g Fiber 6g, Total Sugar 2g; Added Sugar 0g; Protein 6g

no-stir polenta with arugula, figs, and blue cheese

serves 4   **total time** 1 hour 20 minutes

- 1 cup coarse-ground cornmeal
- ½ cup oil-packed sun-dried tomatoes, chopped
- 1 teaspoon minced fresh thyme or ¼ teaspoon dried
- ½ teaspoon table salt
- ¼ teaspoon pepper
- 3 tablespoons extra-virgin olive oil, divided
- 2 ounces (2 cups) baby arugula
- 4 figs, cut into ½-inch-thick wedges
- 1 tablespoon balsamic vinegar
- 2 ounces blue cheese, crumbled (½ cup)
- 2 tablespoons pine nuts, toasted

why this recipe works This Italian-inspired entrée is a study in contrasts: warm, savory polenta topped with a peppery arugula salad, juicy fresh figs, sweet-sour balsamic, and piquant blue cheese. The steam heat gently cooked the polenta for creamy, better-than-stovetop results. Coarse-ground degerminated cornmeal such as yellow grits (with uniform grains the size of couscous) works best in this recipe. Avoid instant or quick-cooking products, as well as whole-grain cornmeal (read the ingredient list on the package to determine this), in this recipe. You will need a 1½-quart round soufflé dish or ceramic dish of similar size for this recipe.

1 Arrange trivet included with Instant Pot in base of insert and add 1 cup water. Fold sheet of aluminum foil into 16 by 6-inch sling, then rest 1½-quart round soufflé dish in center of sling. Whisk 4 cups water, cornmeal, tomatoes, thyme, salt, and pepper together in bowl, then transfer mixture to soufflé dish. Using sling, lower soufflé dish into pot and onto trivet; allow narrow edges of sling to rest along sides of insert.

2 Lock lid in place and close pressure release valve. Select high pressure cook function and cook for 40 minutes. Turn off Instant Pot and quick-release pressure. Carefully remove lid, allowing steam to escape away from you.

3 Using sling, transfer soufflé dish to wire rack. Whisk 1 tablespoon oil into polenta, smoothing out any lumps. Let sit until thickened slightly, about 10 minutes. Season with salt and pepper to taste.

4 Toss arugula and figs with vinegar and remaining 2 tablespoons oil in bowl, and season with salt and pepper to taste. Divide polenta among individual serving plates and top with arugula mixture, blue cheese, and pine nuts. Serve.

per serving
Cal 360; Total Fat 21g; Sat Fat 4.5g; Chol 10mg; Sodium 510mg; Total Carbs 38g, Fiber 8g, Total Sugar 9g; Added Sugar 0g; Protein 7g

wild mushroom farrotto

serves 4 to 6   **total time** 1 hour

1½ cups whole farro

3 tablespoons extra-virgin olive oil, divided, plus extra for drizzling

12 ounces cremini or white mushrooms, trimmed and sliced thin

½ onion, chopped fine

½ teaspoon table salt

¼ teaspoon pepper

1 garlic clove, minced

¼ ounce dried porcini mushrooms, rinsed and chopped fine

2 teaspoons minced fresh thyme or ½ teaspoon dried

¼ cup dry white wine

2½ cups chicken or vegetable broth, plus extra as needed

2 ounces Parmesan cheese, grated (1 cup), plus extra for serving

2 teaspoons lemon juice

½ cup chopped fresh parsley

why this recipe works Farrotto is a robust risotto-style dish swapping in farro for the traditional Arborio rice. Achieving a velvety texture with farro can be a challenge, since much of farro's starch is trapped inside the outer bran. Cracking the farro in a blender freed up enough starch to create the appropriate risotto-like consistency. We used the Instant Pot's sauté function to jump-start meaty mushrooms before adding the cracked farro along with garlic, dried porcinis, thyme, and some white wine for an aromatic backbone. The best part about using the Instant Pot? Once it was under pressure, the cooking was completely hands-off: We could simply add a measured amount of liquid up front—no stirring, no adding broth in stages, no standing by the stove. A healthy heaping of Parmesan cheese at the end made the finished farrotto luxuriously creamy. Do not use quick-cooking, presteamed, or pearl farro (read the ingredient list on the package to determine this) in this recipe. Be sure to use a blender in step 1; the farro will not pulse properly in a food processor.

1 Pulse farro in blender until about half of grains are broken into smaller pieces, about 6 pulses.

2 Using highest sauté function, heat 2 tablespoons oil in Instant Pot until shimmering. Add cremini mushrooms, onion, salt, and pepper, partially cover, and cook until mushrooms are softened and have released their liquid, about 5 minutes. Stir in farro, garlic, porcini mushrooms, and thyme and cook until fragrant, about 1 minute. Stir in wine and cook until nearly evaporated, about 30 seconds. Stir in broth.

3 Lock lid in place and close pressure release valve. Select high pressure cook function and cook for 12 minutes. Turn off Instant Pot and quick-release pressure. Carefully remove lid, allowing steam to escape away from you.

4 If necessary adjust consistency with extra hot broth, or continue to cook farrotto, using highest sauté function, stirring frequently, until proper consistency is achieved. (Farrotto should be slightly thickened, and spoon dragged along bottom of multicooker should leave trail that quickly fills in.)

Add Parmesan and remaining 1 tablespoon oil and stir vigorously until farrotto becomes creamy. Stir in lemon juice and season with salt and pepper to taste. Sprinkle individual portions with parsley and extra Parmesan, and drizzle with extra oil before serving.

per serving
Cal 280; Total Fat 10g; Sat Fat 2.5g; Chol 5mg; Sodium 630mg; Total Carbs 35g, Fiber 4g, Total Sugar 2g; Added Sugar 0g; Protein 13g

barley salad with lemon-tahini dressing

serves 4 to 6   **total time** 1 hour

1½ cups pearl barley

5 tablespoons extra-virgin olive oil, divided

1½ teaspoons table salt, for cooking barley

¼ cup tahini

1 teaspoon grated lemon zest plus ¼ cup juice (2 lemons)

1 tablespoon sumac, divided

1 garlic clove, minced

¾ teaspoon table salt

1 English cucumber, cut into ½-inch pieces

1 carrot, peeled and shredded

1 red bell pepper, stemmed, seeded, and chopped

4 scallions, sliced thin

2 tablespoons finely chopped jarred hot cherry peppers

¼ cup coarsely chopped fresh mint

why this recipe works A simple salad vegetable salad can be found with almost any meal in Israel—its genius lies in the balance of freshness from the region's produce and brightness from the dressing's acidity. However, that salad is not a meal in itself, so we remedied this by adding chewy barley. The barley cooked in a mere 8 minutes under pressure (a huge improvement from the upward of 45 minutes required on the stove), and cooking it pasta-style, in plenty of water, ensured it cooked perfectly and evenly. A bright tahini dressing with olive oil, lemon juice, and fruity sumac brought it all together, and some chopped hot cherry peppers added both a pleasing tang and a slug of heat against the cooling salad. Do not substitute hulled, hull-less, quick-cooking, or presteamed barley (read the ingredient list on the package to determine this) in this recipe.

1   Combine 6 cups water, barley, 1 tablespoon oil, and 1½ teaspoons salt in Instant Pot. Lock lid in place and close pressure release valve. Select high pressure cook function and cook for 8 minutes. Turn off Instant Pot and let pressure release naturally for 15 minutes. Quick-release any remaining pressure, then carefully remove lid, allowing steam to escape away from you. Drain barley, spread onto rimmed baking sheet, and let cool completely, about 15 minutes.

2   Meanwhile, whisk remaining ¼ cup oil, tahini, 2 tablespoons water, lemon zest and juice, 1 teaspoon sumac, garlic, and ¾ teaspoon salt in large bowl until combined; let sit for 15 minutes.

3   Measure out and reserve ½ cup dressing for serving. Add barley, cucumber, carrot, bell pepper, scallions, and cherry peppers to bowl with dressing and gently toss to combine. Season with salt and pepper to taste. Transfer salad to serving dish and sprinkle with mint and remaining 2 teaspoons sumac. Serve, passing reserved dressing separately.

per serving
Cal 370; Total Fat 18g; Sat Fat 2.5g; Chol 0mg; Sodium 510mg; Total Carbs 47g, Fiber 10g, Total Sugar 3g; Added Sugar 0g; Protein 8g

cannellini bean salad

serves 6 to 8   **total time** 1 hour, plus brining time

1½ tablespoons table salt, for brining

1 pound (2½ cups) dried cannellini beans, picked over and rinsed

¼ cup extra-virgin olive oil, divided

¾ teaspoon table salt, divided

¼ cup tahini

3 tablespoons lemon juice

1 tablespoon ground dried Aleppo pepper, plus extra for sprinkling

8 ounces cherry tomatoes, halved

¼ red onion, sliced thin

½ cup fresh parsley leaves

1 recipe hard-cooked eggs, quartered (optional) (page 10)

1 tablespoon toasted sesame seeds

why this recipe works Unlike some of our brothier bean dishes, in which partially broken-down beans offer a welcome thickening starchy texture, for a salad preparation we wanted sturdy beans that could stand up to a dressing and a good stir. Using the gentler low pressure setting ensured our beans were firm but not under-cooked, and completely intact. We also quick-released the pressure and rinsed the beans under cold water to prevent them from overcooking. Tahini, lemon juice, and ground dried Aleppo pepper made a bright dressing, and tomatoes, onion, and parsley contributed to our salad's freshness. The addition of hard-cooked eggs provided extra protein, adding enough substance for the salad to act as a meal as well as a complex and unique side. If you can't find ground dried Aleppo pepper, you can substitute ¾ teaspoon of paprika and ¾ teaspoon of finely chopped red pepper flakes. See page 8 for more information on brining beans.

1 Dissolve 1½ tablespoons salt in 2 quarts cold water in large container. Add beans and soak at room temperature for at least 8 hours or up to 24 hours. Drain and rinse well.

2 Add beans, 8 cups water, 1 tablespoon oil, and ½ teaspoon salt to Instant Pot. Lock lid in place and close pressure release valve. Select low pressure cook function and cook for 3 minutes. Turn off Instant Pot and quick-release pressure. Carefully remove lid, allowing steam to escape away from you. Drain beans, rinse with cold water, and drain again.

3 Meanwhile, whisk remaining 3 tablespoons oil, tahini, lemon juice, Aleppo pepper, 1 tablespoon water, and remaining ¼ teaspoon salt in large bowl until combined; let sit for 15 minutes. Add beans, tomatoes, onion, and parsley and gently toss to combine. Season with salt and pepper to taste. Transfer salad to serving dish and arrange eggs on top, if using. Sprinkle with sesame seeds and extra Aleppo pepper to taste. Serve.

per serving
Cal 340; Total Fat 13g; Sat Fat 2.5g; Chol 105mg; Sodium 330mg; Total Carbs 38g, Fiber 20g, Total Sugar 2g; Added Sugar 0g; Protein 17g

french lentils with swiss chard

serves 6   **total time** 1 hour

2 tablespoons extra-virgin olive oil, plus extra for drizzling

12 ounces Swiss chard, stems chopped fine, leaves sliced into ½-inch-wide strips

1 onion, chopped fine

½ teaspoon table salt

2 garlic cloves, minced

1 teaspoon minced fresh thyme or ¼ teaspoon dried

2½ cups water

1 cup French green lentils, picked over and rinsed

3 tablespoons whole-grain mustard

½ teaspoon grated lemon zest plus 1 teaspoon juice

3 tablespoons sliced almonds, toasted

2 tablespoons chopped fresh parsley

why this recipe works French lentils are a favorite in the Mediterranean thanks to their rich complexity. The quick, even cooking of the Instant Pot ensured the lentils kept their shape and firm-tender texture after cooking under pressure in a garlic-and-thyme-bolstered liquid. After releasing the pressure, we stirred in Swiss chard leaves until just wilted, letting them maintain their fresh bite. A bit of mustard stirred in off the heat added a tangy kick, while almonds and parsley countered with a rich, fresh finish. We prefer French green lentils, or *lentilles du Puy*, for this recipe, but it will work with any type of lentil except red or yellow.

1 Using highest sauté function, heat oil in Instant Pot until shimmering. Add chard stems, onion, and salt and cook until vegetables are softened, about 5 minutes. Stir in garlic and thyme and cook until fragrant, about 30 seconds. Stir in water and lentils.

2 Lock lid in place and close pressure release valve. Select high pressure cook function and cook for 11 minutes. Turn off Instant Pot and let pressure release naturally for 15 minutes. Quick-release any remaining pressure, then carefully remove lid, allowing steam to escape away from you.

3 Stir chard leaves into lentils, 1 handful at a time, and let cook in residual heat until wilted, about 5 minutes. Stir in mustard and lemon zest and juice. Season with salt and pepper to taste. Transfer to serving dish, drizzle with extra oil, and sprinkle with almonds and parsley. Serve.

per serving
Cal 190; Total Fat 8g; Sat Fat 1g; Chol 0mg; Sodium 470mg; Total Carbs 23g, Fiber 6g, Total Sugar 2g; Added Sugar 0g; Protein 9g

greek chickpeas with coriander and sage

serves 6 to 8   **total time** 1 hour, plus brining time

1½ tablespoons table salt,
for brining

1 pound (2½ cups) dried
chickpeas, picked over
and rinsed

2 tablespoons extra-virgin
olive oil, plus extra
for drizzling

2 onions, halved and
sliced thin

¼ teaspoon table salt

1 tablespoon coriander
seeds, cracked

¼–½ teaspoon red pepper flakes

2½ cups chicken broth

¼ cup fresh sage leaves

2 bay leaves

1½ teaspoons grated lemon
zest plus 2 teaspoons juice

2 tablespoons minced
fresh parsley

why this recipe works Often relegated to a supporting role or blitzed into hummus, whole chickpeas rarely are center stage. But here, inspired by slow-baked chickpeas from Greece, the dish is little more than chickpeas, caramelized onions, and some carefully chosen herbs and spices in a superflavorful broth. The chickpeas paired beautifully with some lemony coriander seeds that kept their distinctive character but softened into little bursting pockets of flavor. Sage leaves, mellowed by low pressure cooking, transformed into tender, mild greens that became integral for their subtle yet floral notes. See page 8 for more information on brining beans. To crack coriander, place the seeds on a cutting board and rock the bottom edge of a skillet over them until they crack.

1 Dissolve 1½ tablespoons salt in 2 quarts cold water in large container. Add chickpeas and soak at room temperature for at least 8 hours or up to 24 hours. Drain and rinse well.

2 Using highest sauté function, heat oil in Instant Pot until shimmering. Add onions and ¼ teaspoon salt and cook until onions are softened and well browned, 10 to 12 minutes. Stir in coriander and pepper flakes and cook until fragrant, about 30 seconds. Stir in broth, scraping up any browned bits, then stir in chickpeas, sage, and bay leaves.

3 Lock lid in place and close pressure release valve. Select low pressure cook function and cook for 10 minutes. Turn off Instant Pot and let pressure release naturally for 15 minutes. Quick-release any remaining pressure, then carefully remove lid, allowing steam to escape away from you.

4 Discard bay leaves. Stir lemon zest and juice into chickpeas and season with salt and pepper to taste. Sprinkle with parsley. Serve, drizzling individual portions with extra oil.

per serving
Cal 190; Total Fat 6g; Sat Fat 0.5g; Chol 0mg; Sodium 360mg; Total Carbs 40g, Fiber 1g, Total Sugar 3g; Added Sugar 0g; Protein 11g

moroccan white beans with lamb

serves 6 to 8   **total time** 1 hour 15 minutes, plus brining time

---

1½ tablespoons table salt,
   for brining

1 pound (2½ cups) dried
   great Northern beans,
   picked over and rinsed

1 (12-ounce) lamb shoulder
   chop (blade or round bone),
   ¾ to 1 inch thick, trimmed
   and halved

½ teaspoon table salt

2 tablespoons extra-virgin
   olive oil, plus extra
   for serving

1 onion, chopped

1 red bell pepper, stemmed,
   seeded, and chopped

2 tablespoons tomato paste

3 garlic cloves, minced

2 teaspoons paprika

2 teaspoons ground cumin

1½ teaspoons ground ginger

¼ teaspoon cayenne pepper

½ cup dry white wine

2 cups chicken broth

2 tablespoons minced
   fresh parsley

why this recipe works *Loubia* is a dish of stewed white beans that is well loved in Morocco. Traditionally, the beans are cooked in a warm-spiced tomatoey base and scooped up with fluffy pita bread, making for a comforting and complete meal. A small amount of meat is used as seasoning, allowing the beans to shine. We used thrifty lamb shoulder chops here for their easy availability and forgiving cook time (other cuts were tough by the time the beans were ready). We chose dried beans over canned for their superior flavor and texture, leaving us with soft, intact beans and melt-in-your-mouth tender pieces of lamb. Just 1 minute under pressure and then 15 minutes of natural release was perfect for producing beans that were uniformly cooked, as this allowed the beans to cook more gently toward the end. See page 8 for more information on brining beans.

1 Dissolve 1½ tablespoons salt in 2 quarts cold water in large container. Add beans and soak at room temperature for at least 8 hours or up to 24 hours. Drain and rinse well.

2 Pat lamb dry with paper towels and sprinkle with ½ teaspoon salt. Using highest sauté function, heat oil in Instant Pot for 5 minutes (or until just smoking). Brown lamb, about 5 minutes per side; transfer to plate.

3 Add onion and bell pepper to fat left in pot and cook, using highest sauté function, until softened, about 5 minutes. Stir in tomato paste, garlic, paprika, cumin, ginger, and cayenne and cook until fragrant, about 30 seconds. Stir in wine, scraping up any browned bits, then stir in broth and beans.

4 Nestle lamb into beans and add any accumulated juices. Lock lid in place and close pressure release valve. Select high pressure cook function and cook for 1 minute. Turn off Instant Pot and let pressure release naturally for 15 minutes. Quick-release any remaining pressure, then carefully remove lid, allowing steam to escape away from you.

5 Transfer lamb to cutting board, let cool slightly, then shred into bite-size pieces using 2 forks; discard excess fat and bones. Stir lamb and parsley into beans, and season with salt and pepper to taste. Drizzle individual portions with extra oil before serving.

per serving
Cal 350; Total Fat 12g; Sat Fat 4g; Chol 25mg; Sodium 410mg; Total Carbs 40g, Fiber 15g, Total Sugar 2g; Added Sugar 0g; Protein 20g

creamy spring vegetable linguine

serves 4 to 6   **total time** 45 minutes

---

1 pound linguine

5 cups water, plus extra as needed

1 tablespoon extra-virgin olive oil

1 teaspoon table salt

1 cup jarred whole baby artichokes packed in water, quartered

1 cup frozen peas, thawed

4 ounces finely grated Pecorino Romano (2 cups), plus extra for serving

½ teaspoon pepper

2 teaspoons grated lemon zest

2 tablespoons chopped fresh tarragon

why this recipe works This confoundingly uncomplicated pasta dish was a revelation to us: perfectly cooked al dente noodles in a silky sauce with a vibrant mix of vegetables and flavors—but without multiple pots, boiling water, or draining. Linguine was our favored shape—the thicker strands retained their bite in the ultra-high heat of the Instant Pot. After cooking the pasta, we stirred in convenient jarred baby artichokes and frozen peas. By using exactly the right amount of water, we didn't need to drain the pasta; instead we could capture all of the starch that it released. This made it a cinch to emulsify grated Pecorino and the residual cooking liquid into a luscious sauce. Lemon zest and fresh tarragon brightened the dish. Do not substitute other pasta shapes in this dish, as they require different liquid amounts and will not work in this recipe.

1 Loosely wrap half of pasta in dish towel, then press bundle against corner of counter to break noodles into 6-inch lengths; repeat with remaining pasta.

2 Add pasta, water, oil, and salt to Instant Pot, making sure pasta is completely submerged. Lock lid in place and close pressure release valve. Select high pressure cook function and cook for 4 minutes. Turn off Instant Pot and quick-release pressure. Carefully remove lid, allowing steam to escape away from you.

3 Stir artichokes and peas into pasta, cover, and let sit until heated through, about 3 minutes. Gently stir in Pecorino and pepper until cheese is melted and fully combined, 1 to 2 minutes. Adjust consistency with extra hot water as needed. Stir in lemon zest and tarragon, and season with salt and pepper to taste. Serve, passing extra Pecorino separately.

per serving
Cal 390; Total Fat 8g; Sat Fat 3.5g; Chol 20mg; Sodium 680mg; Total Carbs 59g, Fiber 4g, Total Sugar 3g; Added Sugar 0g; Protein 17g

rigatoni with tomatoes and pancetta

serves 4 to 6   **total time** 1 hour

- 4 ounces pancetta, chopped fine

- 1 onion, chopped fine

- ¼ teaspoon table salt

- 3 garlic cloves, minced

- 2 anchovy fillets, rinsed, patted dry, and minced

- 2 teaspoons fennel seeds, lightly cracked

- ¼ teaspoon red pepper flakes

- 1 (28-ounce) can diced tomatoes

- 2 cups chicken broth

- 1½ cups water

- 1 pound rigatoni

- ¼ cup grated Pecorino Romano cheese, plus extra for serving

- 2 tablespoons minced fresh parsley

why this recipe works Cured pork, bolstered by fragrant fennel seeds, doused in a rich tomato sauce with a hint of chile, and served over perfectly al dente pasta, is a southern Italian classic. Inspired by our Creamy Spring Vegetable Linguine (page 74), we set out to create a heartier, more robust pasta meal but with the same level of ease. We rendered the fat from some chopped pancetta using the Instant Pot's sauté function, and used it to soften onion and garlic, imbuing the aromatics with meaty saltiness. Combining fennel and red pepper flakes with the pancetta evoked a spicy Italian sausage but involved just a fraction of the meat, and anchovy fillets added a subtle umami touch. After sweating the aromatics, it was simply a matter of cooking the pasta, tomatoes, and just the right amount of liquid under pressure to ensure our pasta cooked evenly while still maintaining the perfect level of toothsome tenderness. Bacon can be used in place of the pancetta. Do not substitute other pasta shapes in this dish, as they require different liquid amounts and will not work in this recipe. To crack fennel, place the seeds on a cutting board and rock the bottom edge of a skillet over them until they crack. The sauce will look thin at first but will thicken as it sits in step 4.

1 Using highest sauté function, cook pancetta in Instant Pot, stirring often, until browned and fat is well rendered, 6 to 10 minutes. Using slotted spoon, transfer pancetta to paper towel-lined plate; set aside for serving.

2 Add onion and salt to fat left in pot and cook, using highest sauté function, until onion is softened, about 5 minutes. Stir in garlic, anchovies, fennel seeds, and pepper flakes and cook until fragrant, about 1 minute. Stir in tomatoes and their juice, broth, and water, scraping up any browned bits, then stir in pasta.

3 Lock lid in place and close pressure release valve. Select high pressure cook function and cook for 5 minutes. Turn off Instant Pot and quick-release pressure. Carefully remove lid, allowing steam to escape away from you.

4 Stir in Pecorino and season with salt and pepper to taste. Transfer to serving dish and let sit until sauce thickens slightly, about 5 minutes. Sprinkle with parsley and reserved pancetta. Serve, passing extra Pecorino separately.

per serving
Cal 400; Total Fat 8g; Sat Fat 2.5g; Chol 15mg; Sodium 1020mg; Total Carbs 64g, Fiber 6g, Total Sugar 6g; Added Sugar 0g; Protein 17g

grains, beans, and pasta   77

orecchiette with broccoli rabe and sausage

serves 4 to 6   **total time** 45 minutes

2 tablespoons extra-virgin olive oil, divided

1 pound broccoli rabe, trimmed and cut into 1½-inch pieces

¼ teaspoon table salt

8 ounces hot or sweet Italian sausage, casings removed

6 garlic cloves, minced

¼ teaspoon red pepper flakes

¼ cup dry white wine

4½ cups chicken broth

1 pound orecchiette

2 ounces Parmesan cheese, grated (1 cup), plus extra for serving

why this recipe works "Little ear" pasta with slightly bitter broccoli rabe and fennel seed–scented sausage is found on many a dinner table in the southern province of Puglia, Italy. To keep the broccoli rabe from overcooking and losing its vibrant green color, we sautéed it briefly in the Instant Pot and then set it aside to stir into the pasta right before serving. We then browned Italian sausage and aromatics in the pot before adding our pasta and chicken broth. Cooked at pressure, the orecchiette absorbed most of the flavorful broth. The small amount of broth left in the pot transformed into a smooth sauce once the Parmesan was stirred in, and the orecchiette's curved shape scooped up the sauce, nestling against the bits of savory sausage and crisp-tender broccoli rabe. Do not substitute other pasta shapes in this dish, as they require different liquid amounts and will not work in this recipe.

1 Using highest sauté function, heat 1 tablespoon oil in Instant Pot until shimmering. Add broccoli rabe and salt, partially cover, and cook, stirring occasionally, until broccoli rabe is softened, 3 to 5 minutes. Using slotted spoon, transfer broccoli rabe to bowl; set aside.

2 Add sausage and remaining 1 tablespoon oil to now-empty pot. Using highest sauté function, cook sausage, breaking up meat with wooden spoon, until lightly browned, about 5 minutes. Stir in garlic and pepper flakes and cook until fragrant, about 30 seconds. Stir in wine, scraping up any browned bits, then stir in broth and pasta.

3 Lock lid in place and close pressure release valve. Select high pressure cook function and cook for 4 minutes. Turn off Instant Pot and quick-release pressure. Carefully remove lid, allowing steam to escape away from you.

4 Stir broccoli rabe and any accumulated juices and Parmesan into pasta. Season with salt and pepper to taste. Serve, passing extra Parmesan separately.

per serving
Cal 440; Total Fat 13g; Sat Fat 3.5g; Chol 20mg; Sodium 930mg; Total Carbs 59g, Fiber 1g, Total Sugar 2g; Added Sugar 0g; Protein 22g

couscous with chicken, fennel, and peppers

serves 4 to 6   **total time** 1 hour

---

2 teaspoons ground fenugreek

½ teaspoon table salt

½ teaspoon pepper

½ teaspoon ground cardamom

¼ cup extra-virgin olive oil, divided, plus extra for serving

1 pound ground chicken

1 onion, chopped

1 fennel bulb, 2 tablespoons fronds chopped, stalks discarded, bulb halved, cored, and cut into ½-inch pieces

1½ cups pearl couscous

3 garlic cloves, minced

2¼ cups chicken broth

1 cup jarred roasted red peppers, sliced ¼ inch thick

¼ cup walnuts, toasted and chopped coarse

2 tablespoons chopped fresh parsley

why this recipe works In this Israeli-inspired dish, we seasoned some ground chicken with slightly sweet fenugreek and floral cardamom and sautéed it in the Instant Pot, creating a fond in which we cooked fennel and toasted pearl, or Israeli, couscous. After deglazing the pot with broth, we cooked it all under pressure until the couscous plumped up. Smoky roasted red peppers added complexity, and walnuts brought a pleasing crunch. Be sure to use ground chicken, not ground chicken breast (also labeled 99 percent fat free) in this recipe. Do not substitute regular couscous in this dish, as it requires a different cooking method and will not work in this recipe.

1 Combine fenugreek, salt, pepper, and cardamom in bowl. Using highest sauté function, heat 2 tablespoons oil in Instant Pot until shimmering. Add chicken and 1 teaspoon spice mixture and cook, breaking up any large chicken pieces with wooden spoon, until no longer pink, 5 to 7 minutes. Using slotted spoon, transfer chicken to separate bowl.

2 Add onion, fennel pieces, and remaining 2 tablespoons oil to fat left in pot and cook, using highest sauté function, until vegetables are softened, 6 to 8 minutes. Add couscous and cook, stirring frequently, until lightly browned, about 3 minutes. Stir in garlic and remaining spice mixture and cook until fragrant, about 1 minute.

3 Stir in broth, scraping up any browned bits. Lock lid in place and close pressure release valve. Select high pressure cook function and cook for 4 minutes. Turn off Instant Pot and quick-release pressure. Carefully remove lid, allowing steam to escape away from you.

4 Stir in red peppers and chicken and any accumulated juices. Season with salt and pepper to taste. Transfer to serving dish. Sprinkle with walnuts, parsley, and fennel fronds, and drizzle with extra oil. Serve.

per serving
Cal 430; Total Fat 19g; Sat Fat 3.5g; Chol 50mg; Sodium 590mg; Total Carbs 44g, Fiber 5g, Total Sugar 5g; Added Sugar 0g; Protein 20g

toasted orzo with shrimp and feta

serves 4 to 6   **total time** 1 hour

1 pound large shrimp (26 to 30 per pound), peeled and deveined

1 tablespoon grated lemon zest plus 1 tablespoon juice

¼ teaspoon table salt

¼ teaspoon pepper

2 tablespoons extra-virgin olive oil, plus extra for serving

1 onion, chopped fine

2 garlic cloves, minced

2 cups orzo

2 cups chicken broth, plus extra as needed

1¼ cups water

½ cup pitted kalamata olives, chopped coarse

1 ounce feta cheese, crumbled (¼ cup), plus extra for serving

1 tablespoon chopped fresh dill

why this recipe works In Greece, small, chewy orzo is prized for its ability to turn creamy and absorb flavor, and is used as a base for all types of proteins. We think it pairs particularly well with succulent shrimp. Onion and garlic provided an aromatic base, and toasting the orzo helped coat it with oil, ensuring that each grain remained separate and distinct. Nestling the shrimp into the finished orzo and letting them cook through off the heat eliminated the risk of overcooking them. Kalamata olives were a perfect salty counterpoint to the toasty orzo and lemony shrimp, and a judicious amount of feta cheese added some tang and just enough richness. Do not substitute larger shrimp here; they will not cook through in time.

1   Toss shrimp with lemon zest, salt, and pepper in bowl; refrigerate until ready to use.

2   Using highest sauté function, heat oil in Instant Pot until shimmering. Add onion and cook until softened, about 5 minutes. Stir in garlic and cook until fragrant, about 30 seconds. Add orzo and cook, stirring frequently, until orzo is coated with oil and lightly browned, about 5 minutes. Stir in broth and water, scraping up any browned bits.

3   Lock lid in place and close pressure release valve. Select high pressure cook function and cook for 2 minutes. Turn off Instant Pot and quick-release pressure. Carefully remove lid, allowing steam to escape away from you.

4   Stir shrimp, olives, and feta into orzo. Cover and let sit until shrimp are opaque throughout, 5 to 7 minutes. Adjust consistency with extra hot broth as needed. Stir in dill and lemon juice, and season with salt and pepper to taste. Sprinkle individual portions with extra feta and drizzle with extra oil before serving.

per serving
Cal 320; Total Fat 8g; Sat Fat 2g; Chol 75mg; Sodium 670mg; Total Carbs 46g, Fiber 2g, Total Sugar 4g; Added Sugar 0g; Protein 18g

fish and shellfish

poached salmon

serves 4   **total time** 30 minutes

---

1 lemon, sliced ¼ inch thick

4 (6-ounce) skinless salmon fillets, 1½ inches thick

½ teaspoon table salt

¼ teaspoon pepper

why this recipe works We love salmon for its light texture and versatility—it's equally at home on the dinner table or as a part of an elegant brunch spread. (And don't even get us started about its laundry list of health benefits!) But cooking this popular fish can be intimidating, since it overcooks and dries out so easily. Enter the Instant Pot—with its consistent moisture level and temperature, plus its precise timing, foolproof results are easy to get every time. A mere ½ cup of water in the bottom of the pot was plenty to poach our fish to perfection. A foil sling made it easy to transfer the cooked salmon from pot to serving plate, while a few lemon slices under the salmon added a bit of brightness and insulated the fish from the direct heat. This recipe works best with farmed salmon; we do not recommend using wild salmon here, as it is much leaner. The salmon should register about 125 degrees (for medium-rare) after cooking; if it doesn't, partially cover the pot with the lid and continue to cook using the highest sauté function until the desired temperature is achieved. Serve with Tzatziki (page 17) or Olive Tapenade (page 18), if desired.

1   Add ½ cup water to Instant Pot. Fold sheet of aluminum foil into 16 by 6-inch sling. Arrange lemon slices widthwise in 2 rows across center of sling. Sprinkle flesh side of salmon with salt and pepper, then arrange skinned side down on top of lemon slices.

2   Using sling, lower salmon into Instant Pot; allow narrow edges of sling to rest along sides of insert. Lock lid in place and close pressure release valve. Select high pressure cook function and cook for 3 minutes.

3   Turn off Instant Pot and quick-release pressure. Carefully remove lid, allowing steam to escape away from you. Using sling, transfer salmon to large plate. Gently lift and tilt fillets with spatula to remove lemon slices. Serve.

per serving
Cal 350; Total Fat 23g; Sat Fat 5g; Chol 95mg; Sodium 390mg; Total Carbs 0g, Fiber 0g, Total Sugar 0g; Added Sugar 0g; Protein 35g

salmon with lemon-garlic mashed cauliflower

serves 4   **total time** 1 hour

- 2 tablespoons extra-virgin olive oil

- 4 garlic cloves, peeled and smashed

- ½ cup chicken or vegetable broth

- ¾ teaspoon table salt, divided

- 1 large head cauliflower (3 pounds), cored and cut into 2-inch florets

- 4 (6-ounce) skinless salmon fillets, 1½ inches thick

- ½ teaspoon ras el hanout

- ½ teaspoon grated lemon zest

- 3 scallions, sliced thin

- 1 tablespoon sesame seeds, toasted

why this recipe works Here, a mild, smooth mash of cauliflower forms the perfect base for salmon fillets rubbed with *ras el hanout*, an aromatic North African blend of warm spices. We loved that the Instant Pot synced the cooking times of the cauliflower and salmon, so it was simply a matter of using a foil sling to separate the two to make cooking and serving as straightforward as possible. We started by blooming a generous amount of garlic, and then we added the cauliflower and a small amount of broth before placing the salmon in the pot. After the salmon cooked under pressure for a mere 2 minutes, we removed it and mashed the cauliflower right in the pot, adding lemon zest at the end for a sweetly floral punch. This recipe works best with farmed salmon; we do not recommend using wild salmon here, as it is much leaner. The salmon should register about 125 degrees (for medium-rare) after cooking; if it doesn't, partially cover the pot with the lid and continue to cook using the highest sauté function until the desired temperature is achieved. You can find ras el hanout in the spice aisle of most well-stocked supermarkets.

1 Using highest sauté function, cook oil and garlic in Instant Pot until garlic is fragrant and light golden brown, about 3 minutes. Turn off Instant Pot, then stir in broth and ¼ teaspoon salt. Arrange cauliflower in pot in even layer.

2 Fold sheet of aluminum foil into 16 by 6-inch sling. Sprinkle flesh side of salmon with ras el hanout and remaining ½ teaspoon salt, then arrange skinned side down in center of sling. Using sling, lower salmon into Instant Pot on top of cauliflower; allow narrow edges of sling to rest along sides of insert. Lock lid in place and close pressure release valve. Select high pressure cook function and cook for 2 minutes.

3 Turn off Instant Pot and quick-release pressure. Carefully remove lid, allowing steam to escape away from you. Using sling, transfer salmon to large plate. Tent with foil and let rest while finishing cauliflower.

4 Using potato masher, mash cauliflower mixture until no large chunks remain. Using highest sauté function, cook cauliflower, stirring often, until slightly thickened, about 3 minutes. Stir in lemon zest and season with salt and pepper to taste. Serve salmon with cauliflower, sprinkling individual portions with scallions and sesame seeds.

per serving
Cal 480; Total Fat 31g; Sat Fat 6g; Chol 95mg; Sodium 650mg; Total Carbs 9g, Fiber 3g, Total Sugar 3g; Added Sugar 0g; Protein 38g

salmon with garlicky broccoli rabe and white beans

serves 4   **total time** 45 minutes

- 2 tablespoons extra-virgin olive oil, plus extra for drizzling

- 4 garlic cloves, sliced thin

- ½ cup chicken or vegetable broth

- ¼ teaspoon red pepper flakes

- 1 lemon, sliced ¼ inch thick, plus lemon wedges for serving

- 4 (6-ounce) skinless salmon fillets, 1½ inches thick

- ½ teaspoon table salt

- ¼ teaspoon pepper

- 1 pound broccoli rabe, trimmed and cut into 1-inch pieces

- 1 (15-ounce) can cannellini beans, rinsed

why this recipe works One of the most appealing attributes of the Instant Pot is the ease with which you can switch between cooking functions to effortlessly create the best cooking environment for each element of a meal—all in one vessel. We started off using the sauté function to make delicate, aromatic garlic chips for a garnish, adding a crispy, slightly sweet element to the finished dish. Then we switched to high pressure to cook our salmon fillets before removing them and returning to the sauté function to briefly simmer broccoli rabe and cannellini beans to tender perfection in the remaining liquid. A drizzle of olive oil, and dinner was on the table. This recipe works best with farmed salmon; we do not recommend using wild salmon here, as it is much leaner. The salmon should register about 125 degrees (for medium-rare) after cooking; if it doesn't, partially cover the pot with the lid and continue to cook using the highest sauté function until the desired temperature is achieved.

1   Using highest sauté function, cook oil and garlic in Instant Pot until garlic is fragrant and light golden brown, about 3 minutes. Using slotted spoon, transfer garlic to paper towel-lined plate and season with salt to taste; set aside for serving. Turn off Instant Pot, then stir in broth and pepper flakes.

2   Fold sheet of aluminum foil into 16 by 6-inch sling. Arrange lemon slices widthwise in 2 rows across center of sling. Sprinkle flesh side of salmon with salt and pepper, then arrange skinned side down on top of lemon slices. Using sling, lower salmon into Instant Pot; allow narrow edges of sling to rest along sides of insert. Lock lid in place and close pressure release valve. Select high pressure cook function and cook for 3 minutes.

3   Turn off Instant Pot and quick-release pressure. Carefully remove lid, allowing steam to escape away from you. Using sling, transfer salmon to large plate. Tent with foil and let rest while preparing broccoli rabe mixture.

4   Stir broccoli rabe and beans into cooking liquid, partially cover, and cook, using highest sauté function, until broccoli rabe is tender, about 5 minutes. Season with salt and pepper to taste. Gently lift and tilt salmon fillets with spatula to remove lemon slices. Serve salmon with broccoli rabe mixture and lemon wedges, sprinkling individual portions with garlic chips and drizzling with extra oil.

per serving
Cal 510; Total Fat 30g; Sat Fat 6g; Chol 95mg; Sodium 650mg; Total Carbs 15g, Fiber 6g, Total Sugar 2g; Added Sugar 0g; Protein 43g

salmon with wild rice and orange salad

serves 4   **total time** 1 hour 15 minutes

1 cup wild rice, picked over and rinsed

3 tablespoons extra-virgin olive oil, divided

1½ teaspoon table salt, for cooking rice

2 oranges, plus ⅛ teaspoon grated orange zest

4 (6-ounce) skinless salmon fillets, 1½ inches thick

1 teaspoon ground dried Aleppo pepper

½ teaspoon table salt

1 small shallot, minced

1 tablespoon red wine vinegar

2 teaspoons Dijon mustard

1 teaspoon honey

2 carrots, peeled and shredded

¼ cup chopped fresh mint

why this recipe works Despite its name, wild rice is actually an aquatic grass—we love it for its high nutritional value and woodsy smokiness. The only downside? It can take nearly an hour to cook. The Instant Pot slashed that time, cooking it in just 15 minutes, giving us time to prepare additional ingredients for a vibrant, citrusy rice salad studded with juicy oranges and sweet shredded carrots. A generous sprinkling of ground dried Aleppo pepper gave our salmon a uniquely fruity touch of heat that complemented the nutty, citrusy, and herbal flavors in the salad. This recipe works best with farmed salmon; we do not recommend using wild salmon here, as it is much leaner. The salmon should register about 125 degrees (for medium-rare) after cooking; if it doesn't, partially cover the pot with the lid and continue to cook using the highest sauté function until the desired temperature is achieved. Do not use quick-cooking or presteamed wild rice in this recipe. If you can't find ground dried Aleppo pepper, you can substitute ¾ teaspoon paprika plus ¼ teaspoon finely chopped red pepper flakes.

1 Combine 6 cups water, rice, 1 tablespoon oil, and 1½ teaspoons salt in Instant Pot. Lock lid in place and close pressure release valve. Select high pressure cook function and cook for 15 minutes. Turn off Instant Pot and let pressure release naturally for 15 minutes. Quick-release any remaining pressure, then carefully remove lid, allowing steam to escape away from you. Drain rice and set aside to cool slightly. Wipe pot clean with paper towels.

2 Add ½ cup water to now-empty Instant Pot. Fold sheet of aluminum foil into 16 by 6-inch sling. Slice 1 orange ¼ inch thick and shingle widthwise in 3 rows across center of sling. Sprinkle flesh side of salmon with Aleppo pepper and ½ teaspoon salt, then arrange skinned side down on top of orange slices. Using sling, lower salmon into Instant Pot; allow narrow edges of sling to rest along sides of insert. Lock lid in place and close pressure release valve. Select high pressure cook function and cook for 3 minutes.

3 Meanwhile, cut away peel and pith from remaining 1 orange. Quarter orange, then slice crosswise into ¼-inch pieces. Whisk remaining 2 tablespoons oil, shallot, vinegar, mustard, honey, and orange zest together in large bowl. Add rice, orange pieces, carrots, and mint, and gently toss to combine. Season with salt and pepper to taste.

4 Turn off Instant Pot and quick-release pressure. Carefully remove lid, allowing steam to escape away from you. Using sling, transfer salmon to large plate. Gently lift and tilt fillets with spatula to remove orange slices. Serve salmon with salad.

per serving
Cal 690; Total Fat 34g; Sat Fat 7g; Chol 95mg; Sodium 770mg; Total Carbs 51g, Fiber 5g, Total Sugar 8g; Added Sugar 1g; Protein 43g

cod with warm beet and arugula salad

serves 4   **total time** 1 hour

¼ cup extra-virgin olive oil, divided, plus extra for drizzling

1 shallot, sliced thin

2 garlic cloves, minced

1½ pounds small beets, scrubbed, trimmed, and cut into ½-inch wedges

½ cup chicken or vegetable broth

1 tablespoon dukkah, plus extra for sprinkling

¼ teaspoon table salt

4 (6-ounce) skinless cod fillets, 1½ inches thick

1 tablespoon lemon juice

2 ounces (2 cups) baby arugula

why this recipe works Since delicate fish fillets cook so quickly in the Instant Pot, we were pleased to discover that we could stagger the cooking times of different ingredients and still create a full meal in under an hour. We love the combination of sweet, earthy beets and light, buttery cod, and so we started by braising our beets in just 3 minutes under pressure—a process that can otherwise take up to an hour. What's more, the intense heat of the Instant Pot rendered the nutrient-packed skins of our unpeeled beets utterly undetectable. Next, we created a foil sling on which to suspend our cod atop the beets and cooked both for just 2 minutes. Arugula, a lemony dressing, and a sprinkling of *dukkah*—a crunchy, flavor-packed Egyptian condiment—brought it all together. Look for beets measuring approximately 2 inches in diameter. Haddock and striped bass are good substitutes for the cod. Thin tail-end fillets can be folded to achieve proper thickness. The cod should register about 135 degrees after cooking; if it doesn't, partially cover the pot with the lid and continue to cook using the highest sauté function until the desired temperature is achieved. We prefer to make our own Dukkah (page 19), but any store-bought variety will work.

1   Using highest sauté function, heat 1 tablespoon oil in Instant Pot until shimmering. Add shallot and cook until softened, about 2 minutes. Stir in garlic and cook until fragrant, about 30 seconds. Stir in beets and broth. Lock lid in place and close pressure release valve. Select high pressure cook function and cook for 3 minutes. Turn off Instant Pot and quick-release pressure. Carefully remove lid, allowing steam to escape away from you.

2   Fold sheet of aluminum foil into 16 by 6-inch sling. Combine 2 tablespoons oil, dukkah, and salt in bowl, then brush cod with oil mixture. Arrange cod skinned side down in center of sling. Using sling, lower cod into Instant Pot; allow narrow edges of sling to rest along sides of insert. Lock lid in place and close pressure release valve. Select high pressure cook function and cook for 2 minutes.

3 Turn off Instant Pot and quick-release pressure. Carefully remove lid, allowing steam to escape away from you. Using sling, transfer cod to large plate. Tent with foil and let rest while finishing beet salad.

4 Combine lemon juice and remaining 1 tablespoon oil in large bowl. Using slotted spoon, transfer beets to bowl with oil mixture. Add arugula and gently toss to combine. Season with salt and pepper to taste. Serve cod with salad, sprinkling individual portions with extra dukkah and drizzling with extra oil.

per serving
Cal 340; Total Fat 16g; Sat Fat 2.5g; Chol 75mg; Sodium 460mg; Total
Carbs 14g, Fiber 4g, Total Sugar 9g; Added Sugar 0g; Protein 33g

hake in saffron broth

serves 4   **total time** 1 hour

- 2 tablespoons extra-virgin olive oil, divided, plus extra for drizzling

- 1 onion, chopped

- 4 ounces Spanish-style chorizo sausage, sliced ¼ inch thick

- 4 garlic cloves, minced

- 1 (8-ounce) bottle clam juice

- ¾ cup water

- ½ cup dry white wine

- 8 ounces small red potatoes, unpeeled, quartered

- ¼ teaspoon saffron threads, crumbled

- 1 bay leaf

- 4 (6-ounce) skinless hake fillets, 1½ inches thick

- ½ teaspoon table salt

- ¼ teaspoon pepper

- 2 tablespoons minced fresh parsley

why this recipe works Sometimes known as "red gold," saffron is a common spice in Spanish cooking. It's made from the dried stigmas of *crocus sativus* flowers; the stigmas are so delicate they must be painstakingly harvested by hand. (It takes about 200 hours to pick enough stigmas to produce just 1 pound of saffron.) Luckily, a little bit of saffron goes a long way. Here, a mere ¼ teaspoon was plenty to perfume our broth, while Spanish-style chorizo, clam juice, and wine added flavors evocative of the northern Spanish coast. We chose mild hake (a favorite in Spain) as our versatile complement—we loved how the simple but still luxurious fish allowed the saffron to take center stage—and added waxy red potatoes that soaked up the savory, vibrantly colored broth. Use small red potatoes measuring 1 to 2 inches in diameter. Cod and haddock are good substitutes for the hake; decrease the time under pressure to 2 minutes in step 2. The hake should register about 135 degrees after cooking; if it doesn't, partially cover the pot with the lid and continue to cook using the highest sauté function until the desired temperature is achieved.

1 Using highest sauté function, heat 1 tablespoon oil in Instant Pot until shimmering. Add onion and chorizo and cook until onion is softened and lightly browned, 5 to 7 minutes. Stir in garlic and cook until fragrant, about 30 seconds. Stir in clam juice, water, and wine, scraping up any browned bits. Turn off Instant Pot, then stir in potatoes, saffron, and bay leaf.

2 Fold sheet of aluminum foil into 16 by 6-inch sling. Brush hake with remaining 1 tablespoon oil and sprinkle with salt and pepper. Arrange hake skinned side down in center of sling. Using sling, lower hake into Instant Pot on top of potato mixture; allow narrow edges of sling to rest along sides of insert. Lock lid in place and close pressure release valve. Select high pressure cook function and cook for 3 minutes.

3 Turn off Instant Pot and quick-release pressure. Carefully remove lid, allowing steam to escape away from you. Using sling, transfer hake to large plate. Tent with aluminum foil and let rest while finishing potato mixture.

4 Discard bay leaf. Stir parsley into potato mixture and season with salt to taste. Serve cod with potato mixture and broth, drizzling individual portions with extra oil.

per serving
Cal 410; Total Fat 19g; Sat Fat 5g; Chol 100mg; Sodium 880mg; Total Carbs 14g, Fiber 2g, Total Sugar 2g; Added Sugar 0g; Protein 39g

fish and shellfish 97

braised striped bass with zucchini and tomatoes

serves 4   **total time** 1 hour

- 2 tablespoons extra-virgin olive oil, divided, plus extra for drizzling
- 3 zucchini (8 ounces each), halved lengthwise and sliced ¼ inch thick
- 1 onion, chopped
- ¾ teaspoon table salt, divided
- 3 garlic cloves, minced
- 1 teaspoon minced fresh oregano or ¼ teaspoon dried
- ¼ teaspoon red pepper flakes
- 1 (28-ounce) can whole peeled tomatoes, drained with juice reserved, halved
- 1½ pounds skinless striped bass, 1½ inches thick, cut into 2-inch pieces
- ¼ teaspoon pepper
- 2 tablespoons chopped pitted kalamata olives
- 2 tablespoons shredded fresh mint

why this recipe works Greek-style stewed vegetables with help from olives and mint are the perfect companion to a flaky-yet-meaty fish. Halibut and swordfish are good substitutes for the striped bass here. To prevent the striped bass from overcooking, be sure to turn off the Instant Pot as soon as it reaches pressure. The striped bass should register about 130 degrees after cooking; if it doesn't, partially cover the pot with the lid and continue to cook using the highest sauté function until the desired temperature is achieved.

1 Using highest sauté function, heat 1 tablespoon oil in Instant Pot for 5 minutes (or until just smoking). Add zucchini and cook until tender, about 5 minutes; transfer to bowl and set aside.

2 Add remaining 1 tablespoon oil, onion, and ¼ teaspoon salt to now-empty pot and cook, using highest sauté function, until onion is softened, about 5 minutes. Stir in garlic, oregano, and pepper flakes and cook until fragrant, about 30 seconds. Stir in tomatoes and reserved juice.

3 Sprinkle bass with remaining ½ teaspoon salt and pepper. Nestle bass into tomato mixture and spoon some of cooking liquid on top of pieces. Lock lid in place and close pressure release valve. Select high pressure cook function and set cook time for 0 minutes. Once Instant Pot has reached pressure, immediately turn off pot and quick-release pressure. Carefully remove lid, allowing steam to escape away from you.

4 Transfer bass to plate, tent with aluminum foil, and let rest while finishing vegetables. Stir zucchini into pot and let sit until heated through, about 5 minutes. Stir in olives and season with salt and pepper to taste. Serve bass with vegetables, sprinkling individual portions with mint and drizzling with extra oil.

per serving
Cal 320; Total Fat 11g; Sat Fat 2g; Chol 70mg; Sodium 1090mg; Total Carbs 19g, Fiber 2g, Total Sugar 10g; Added Sugar 0g; Protein 36g

halibut with carrots, white beans, and chermoula

serves 4   **total time** 45 minutes

1 shallot, sliced thin

1 tablespoon extra-virgin olive oil

2 teaspoons lemon juice

1 pound carrots, peeled

1 (15-ounce) can navy beans, rinsed

½ cup chicken or vegetable broth

4 (6-ounce) skinless halibut fillets, 1½ inches thick

3 tablespoons Chermoula (page 17), divided

¼ teaspoon table salt

1 cup fresh parsley or cilantro leaves

2 tablespoons sliced almonds, toasted

why this recipe works This vibrant dish is full of satisfying contrasts—moist, tender halibut fillets with delicately sweet carrots, white beans, a zesty sauce, and fresh herbs. Because halibut tends to be a more expensive fish, we kept the remaining ingredients pantry friendly. We created a base of carrots and convenient canned beans in a splash of broth, and used a foil sling for our halibut for easy removal. In less than a minute under pressure, our carrots cooked to tender perfection, and the beans and broth mingled with the juices from the fish, creating a saucy consistency that napped the fish. We finished the dish with Chermoula (page 17), a zippy Moroccan sauce made with hefty amounts of cilantro, lemon, garlic, and spices, and topped it with a fresh herb salad. Swordfish is a good substitute for the halibut. To prevent the halibut from overcooking, be sure to turn off the Instant Pot as soon as it reaches pressure. The halibut should register about 130 degrees after cooking; if it doesn't, partially cover the pot with the lid and continue to cook using the highest sauté function until the desired temperature is achieved.

1 Combine shallot, oil, and lemon juice in medium bowl; set aside. Cut carrots into 2-inch lengths. Leave thin pieces whole, halve medium pieces lengthwise, and quarter thick pieces lengthwise. Combine carrots, beans, and broth in Instant Pot.

2 Fold sheet of aluminum foil into 16 by 6-inch sling. Brush halibut with 1 tablespoon Chermoula and sprinkle with salt. Arrange halibut skinned side down in center of sling. Using sling, lower halibut into Instant Pot on top of carrot mixture; allow narrow edges of sling to rest along sides of insert.

3 Lock lid in place and close pressure release valve. Select high pressure cook function and set cook time for 0 minutes. Once Instant Pot has reached pressure, immediately turn off pot and quick-release pressure. Carefully remove lid, allowing steam to escape away from you.

4 Using sling, transfer halibut to large plate. Tent with foil and let rest while finishing carrot mixture. Stir remaining 2 tablespoons Chermoula into carrot mixture and season with salt and pepper to taste.

Add parsley and almonds to bowl with shallot mixture and gently toss to combine. Season with salt and pepper to taste. Serve halibut with carrot mixture, topped with parsley salad.

per serving
Cal 430; Total Fat 18g; Sat Fat 2.5g; Chol 85mg; Sodium 750mg; Total Carbs 28g, Fiber 7g, Total Sugar 6g; Added Sugar 0g; Protein 39g

swordfish with peppers and potatoes

serves 4   **total time** 1 hour

- 2 tablespoons extra-virgin olive oil

- 2 red bell peppers, stemmed, seeded, and cut into ½-inch-wide strips

- 2 green bell peppers, stemmed, seeded, and cut into ½-inch-wide strips

- 1 onion, halved and sliced thin

- 1 teaspoon table salt, divided

- 4 garlic cloves, minced

- 1 tablespoon tomato paste

- 1 teaspoon ground dried Espelette pepper, divided

- 1 (14.5-ounce) can whole peeled tomatoes, drained with ¼ cup juice reserved, chopped coarse

- 1 pound Yukon Gold potatoes, peeled, cut into 1-inch pieces

- 4 (6-ounce) skinless swordfish steaks, 1½ inches thick

- ¼ cup Salsa Verde (page 17)

why this recipe works In the Basque regions of Spain and France, a combination of bell peppers, onions, garlic, and ground dried Espelette pepper is a well-loved companion to a wide variety of proteins. We love it with meaty swordfish steaks. A drizzle of Salsa Verde (page 17) tied the dish together. Halibut is a good substitute for the swordfish. To prevent the swordfish from over-cooking, be sure to turn off the Instant Pot as soon as it reaches pressure. The swordfish should register about 130 degrees after cooking; if it doesn't, partially cover the pot with the lid and continue to cook using the highest sauté function until the desired temperature is achieved. If you can't find ground dried Espelette pepper, substitute ½ teaspoon red pepper flakes plus ½ teaspoon paprika.

1 Using highest sauté function, heat oil in Instant Pot until shimmering. Add bell peppers, onion, and ½ teaspoon salt and cook until vegetables are softened, about 5 minutes. Stir in garlic, tomato paste, and ½ teaspoon Espelette pepper and cook until fragrant, about 30 seconds. Stir in tomatoes and reserved juice, scraping up any browned bits, then stir in potatoes.

2 Sprinkle swordfish with remaining ½ teaspoon salt and remaining ½ teaspoon Espelette pepper. Nestle swordfish into vegetable mixture and spoon some of cooking liquid on top of steaks. Lock lid in place and close pressure release valve. Select high pressure cook function and set cook time for 0 minutes. Once Instant Pot has reached pressure, immediately turn off pot and quick-release pressure. Carefully remove lid, allowing steam to escape away from you.

3 Using spatula, transfer swordfish to serving dish. Tent with aluminum foil and let rest while finishing vegetable mixture. Using highest sauté function, cook vegetable mixture until liquid has thickened slightly, about 2 minutes. Serve swordfish with vegetable mixture, drizzling individual portions with Salsa Verde.

per serving
Cal 540; Total Fat 26g; Sat Fat 5g; Chol 110mg; Sodium 920mg; Total Carbs 26g, Fiber 4g, Total Sugar 8g; Added Sugar 0g; Protein 39g

cod with warm tabbouleh salad

serves 4   **total time** 45 minutes

1 cup medium-grind bulgur, rinsed

1 teaspoon table salt, divided

1 lemon, sliced ¼ inch thick, plus 2 tablespoons juice

4 (6-ounce) skinless cod fillets, 1½ inches thick

3 tablespoons extra-virgin olive oil, divided, plus extra for drizzling

¼ teaspoon pepper

1 small shallot, minced

10 ounces cherry tomatoes, halved

1 cup chopped fresh parsley

½ cup chopped fresh mint

why this recipe works Tabbouleh is a Levantine bulgur salad tossed with a lemony dressing and fresh herbs. Although it's often served at room temperature, we found it to be surprisingly elegant warm (this also cut down on waiting time), and we served it with cod for a complete meal. We started by steaming bulgur on its own in a soufflé dish set into the Instant Pot on the trivet; this allowed us to quickly remove the bulgur when it was done so we could use the then-empty pot to cook the fish. We stirred together our still-warm bulgur with some sweet cherry tomatoes, a generous helping of parsley and mint, and a lemon vinaigrette. Haddock and striped bass are good substitutes for the cod. Thin tail-end fillets can be folded to achieve proper thickness. The cod should register about 135 degrees after cooking; if it doesn't, partially cover the pot with the lid and continue to cook using the highest sauté function until the desired temperature is achieved. You will need a 1½-quart round soufflé dish or ceramic dish of similar size for this recipe.

1 Arrange trivet included with Instant Pot in base of insert and add ½ cup water. Fold sheet of aluminum foil into 16 by 6-inch sling, then rest 1½-quart round soufflé dish in center of sling. Combine 1 cup water, bulgur, and ½ teaspoon salt in dish. Using sling, lower soufflé dish into pot and onto trivet; allow narrow edges of sling to rest along sides of insert.

2 Lock lid in place and close pressure release valve. Select high pressure cook function and cook for 3 minutes. Turn off Instant Pot and quick-release pressure. Carefully remove lid, allowing steam to escape away from you. Using sling, transfer soufflé dish to wire rack; set aside to cool. Remove trivet; do not discard sling or water in pot.

3 Arrange lemon slices widthwise in 2 rows across center of sling. Brush cod with 1 tablespoon oil and sprinkle with remaining ½ teaspoon salt and pepper. Arrange cod skinned side down in even layer on top of lemon slices. Using sling, lower cod into Instant Pot; allow narrow edges of sling to rest along sides of insert. Lock lid in place and close pressure release valve. Select high pressure cook function and cook for 3 minutes.

4 Meanwhile, whisk remaining 2 tablespoons oil, lemon juice, and shallot together in large bowl. Add bulgur, tomatoes, parsley, and mint, and gently toss to combine. Season with salt and pepper to taste.

5 Turn off Instant Pot and quick-release pressure. Carefully remove lid, allowing steam to escape away from you. Using sling, transfer cod to large plate. Gently lift and tilt fillets with spatula to remove lemon slices. Serve cod with salad, drizzling individual portions with extra oil.

per serving
Cal 380; Total Fat 12g; Sat Fat 2g; Chol 75mg; Sodium 690mg; Total Carbs 32g, Fiber 6g, Total Sugar 3g; Added Sugar 0g; Protein 36g

fish tagine

serves 4   **total time** 1 hour

- 2 tablespoons extra-virgin olive oil, plus extra for drizzling

- 1 large onion, halved and sliced ¼ inch thick

- 1 pound carrots, peeled, halved lengthwise, and sliced ¼ inch thick

- 2 (2-inch) strips orange zest, plus 1 teaspoon grated zest

- ¾ teaspoon table salt, divided

- 2 tablespoons tomato paste

- 4 garlic cloves, minced, divided

- 1¼ teaspoons paprika

- 1 teaspoon ground cumin

- ¼ teaspoon red pepper flakes

- ¼ teaspoon saffron threads, crumbled

- 1 (8-ounce) bottle clam juice

- 1½ pounds skinless halibut fillets, 1½ inches thick, cut into 2-inch pieces

- ¼ cup pitted oil-cured black olives, quartered

- 2 tablespoons chopped fresh parsley

- 1 teaspoon sherry vinegar

why this recipe works A traditional North African specialty, a tagine is both the name for a conical cooking vessel and the stew that is cooked inside it. The special shape of a tagine allows steam to condense and drip back down onto the stew, keeping it moist and concentrated, and the Instant Pot created a similar cooking environment. For a Moroccan-style fish tagine with the signature sweet and sour flavors of the region, we used onions, carrots, and tomato paste, which, along with fragrant spices, built the base for the broth. Clam juice created an umami-rich broth in which to braise the halibut, our choice for its firm texture that kept its shape while cooking under pressure. For a salty, sour punch, we stirred in olives and sherry vinegar, while parsley added a nice fresh finish. To prevent the halibut from overcooking, be sure to turn off the Instant Pot as soon as it reaches pressure. Swordfish is a good substitute for the halibut.

1   Using highest sauté function, heat oil in Instant Pot until shimmering. Add onion, carrots, orange zest strips, and ¼ teaspoon salt, and cook until vegetables are softened and lightly browned, 10 to 12 minutes. Stir in tomato paste, three-quarters of garlic, paprika, cumin, pepper flakes, and saffron and cook until fragrant, about 30 seconds. Stir in clam juice, scraping up any browned bits.

2   Sprinkle halibut with remaining ½ teaspoon salt. Nestle halibut into onion mixture and spoon some of cooking liquid on top of pieces. Lock lid in place and close pressure release valve. Select high pressure cook function and set cook time for 0 minutes. Once Instant Pot has reached pressure, immediately turn off pot and quick-release pressure.

3   Discard orange zest. Gently stir in olives, parsley, vinegar, grated orange zest, and remaining garlic. Season with salt and pepper to taste. Drizzle extra oil over individual portions before serving.

per serving
Cal 310; Total Fat 15g; Sat Fat 2.5g; Chol 85mg; Sodium 820mg; Total Carbs 18g, Fiber 4g, Total Sugar 8g; Added Sugar 0g; Protein 34g

shrimp with tomatoes and warm spices

serves 4   **total time** 1 hour 15 minutes

1 pound large shrimp
(26 to 30 per pound),
peeled and deveined

2 tablespoons extra-virgin
olive oil, divided, plus extra
for drizzling

5 garlic cloves, minced,
divided

1 teaspoon grated lemon zest

½ teaspoon table salt, divided

⅛ teaspoon pepper

1 red or green bell pepper,
stemmed, seeded, and
chopped

1 small onion, chopped

1 tablespoon ras el hanout

½ teaspoon ground ginger

1 (28-ounce) can whole
peeled tomatoes, drained
with juice reserved,
chopped coarse

¼ cup pitted brine-cured
green or black olives,
chopped coarse

2 tablespoons coarsely
chopped fresh parsley

2 scallions, sliced thin on bias

why this recipe works Succulent shrimp swimming in roasty peppers and tomatoes and flavored by the potent warm spice blend *ras el hanout* is our idea of elevated comfort food. Cooked under pressure, the vegetables softened and their flavor intensi-fied. The shrimp gently cooked in the residual heat of the cooked tomato mixture. Olives provided tangy saltiness, and scallions and a drizzle of extra-virgin olive oil provided a fresh, rich finish. Do not substitute larger shrimp here; they will not cook through in time. Serve over rice or couscous. You can find ras el hanout in the spice aisle of most well-stocked supermarkets.

1   Toss shrimp with 1 tablespoon oil, 1 teaspoon garlic, lemon zest, ¼ teaspoon salt, and pepper; refrigerate until ready to use.

2   Using highest sauté function, heat remaining 1 tablespoon oil in Instant Pot until shimmering. Add bell pepper, onion, and remaining ¼ teaspoon salt and cook until vegetables are softened, about 5 minutes. Stir in remaining garlic, ras el hanout, and ginger and cook until fragrant, about 30 seconds. Stir in tomatoes and reserved juice.

3   Lock lid in place and close pressure release valve. Select high pressure cook function and cook for 15 minutes. Turn off Instant Pot and quick-release pressure. Carefully remove lid, allowing steam to escape away from you.

4   Stir shrimp into tomato mixture, cover, and let sit until opaque throughout, 5 to 7 minutes. Stir in olives and parsley and season with salt and pepper to taste. Sprinkle individual portions with scallions and drizzle with extra oil before serving.

per serving
Cal 210; Total Fat 9g; Sat Fat 1.5g; Chol 105mg; Sodium 970mg; Total
Carbs 16g, Fiber 4g, Total Sugar 7g; Added Sugar 0g; Protein 14g

shrimp and asparagus risotto

serves 4   **total time** 1 hour

¼ cup extra-virgin olive oil, divided

8 ounces asparagus, trimmed and cut on bias into 1-inch lengths

½ onion, chopped fine

¼ teaspoon table salt

1½ cups Arborio rice

3 garlic cloves, minced

½ cup dry white wine

3 cups chicken or vegetable broth, plus extra as needed

1 pound large shrimp (26 to 30 per pound), peeled and deveined

2 ounces Parmesan cheese, grated (1 cup)

1 tablespoon lemon juice

1 tablespoon minced fresh chives

why this recipe works This risotto is bursting with springtime freshness and contrasting textures against a lush backdrop of creamy Arborio rice. While labor-intensive risotto is often relegated to special-occasion menus, the Instant Pot's concentrated, moist heat and closed cooking environment helps you achieve luxurious risotto any day of the week. We started by using the sauté function to briefly cook the asparagus and setting it aside to ensure it stayed al dente. We then sautéed the onion and toasted the rice before adding wine and broth. After releasing the pressure, we stirred the asparagus and shrimp into the fully cooked risotto. The shrimp steamed gently in the warm rice, achieving flawlessly tender results. Parmesan added to the velvety texture, and chives provided a nice bright finish. Arborio rice, which is high in starch, gives risotto its characteristic creaminess; do not substitute other types of rice. Do not substitute larger shrimp here; they will not cook through in time.

1   Using highest sauté function, heat 1 tablespoon oil in Instant Pot until shimmering. Add asparagus, partially cover, and cook until just crisp-tender, about 4 minutes. Using slotted spoon, transfer asparagus to bowl; set aside.

2   Add onion, 2 tablespoons oil, and salt to now-empty pot and cook, using highest sauté function, until onion is softened, about 5 minutes. Stir in rice and garlic and cook until grains are translucent around edges, about 3 minutes. Stir in wine and cook until nearly evaporated, about 1 minute.

3   Stir in broth, scraping up any rice that sticks to bottom of pot. Lock lid in place and close pressure release valve. Select high pressure cook function and cook for 7 minutes.

4   Turn off Instant Pot and quick-release pressure. Carefully remove lid, allowing steam to escape away from you. Stir shrimp and asparagus into risotto, cover, and let sit until shrimp are opaque throughout, 5 to 7 minutes. Add Parmesan and remaining 1 tablespoon oil, and stir vigorously until risotto becomes creamy. Adjust consistency with extra hot broth as needed. Stir in lemon juice and season with salt and pepper to taste. Sprinkle individual portions with chives before serving.

per serving

Cal 540; Total Fat 21g; Sat Fat 4g; Chol 115mg; Sodium 1310mg; Total Carbs 58g, Fiber 2g, Total Sugar 2g; Added Sugar 0g; Protein 27g

clams with brothy rice

serves 4   **total time** 1 hour

---

2 tablespoons extra-virgin olive oil

1 leek, ends trimmed, leek halved lengthwise, sliced 1 inch thick, and washed thoroughly

1 green bell pepper, stemmed, seeded, and chopped fine

1½ cups Arborio rice

3 garlic cloves, minced

½ cup dry white wine

5 cups chicken or vegetable broth, divided

2 pounds littleneck clams, scrubbed

1 cup frozen peas, thawed

1 cup jarred whole baby artichoke hearts packed in water, quartered, rinsed, and patted dry

½ cup Salsa Verde (page 17)

why this recipe works This rice dish from Spain's Mediterranean coast combines the meaty sweetness of clams and their liquor with the verdant flavors of springtime vegetables. Unlike a paella-style rice, in which the rice absorbs most or all of the cooking liquid, brothy rice has a higher proportion of liquid to rice, so that the finished rice remains surrounded by flavorful broth. We built an aromatic base using leek and green bell pepper, and toasted the rice with garlic to enhance its flavor before deglazing the pot with some wine. We added ample broth and clams, and after just 1 minute under pressure our clams had popped open and our rice was perfectly soft. To pack even more vegetables into this one-pot meal, we stirred in convenient jarred artichokes and thawed frozen peas. To emphasize these vegetal flavors and the acidity of the wine, we drizzled everything with a bright Salsa Verde (page 17). Arborio rice, which is high in starch, gives this dish its characteristic creaminess; do not substitute other types of rice. While we prefer the flavor and texture of jarred whole baby artichoke hearts, you can substitute 6 ounces frozen artichoke hearts, thawed and patted dry. Discard any raw clams with an unpleasant odor or with a cracked or broken shell that won't close.

1 Using highest sauté function, heat oil in Instant Pot until shimmering. Add leek and bell pepper and cook until softened, about 8 minutes. Stir in rice and garlic and cook until grains are translucent around edges, about 3 minutes. Stir in wine and cook until nearly evaporated, about 1 minute.

2 Stir in 3 cups broth, scraping up any rice that sticks to bottom of pot, then nestle clams into rice mixture. Lock lid in place and close pressure release valve. Select high pressure cook function and cook for 1 minute.

3 Turn off Instant Pot and quick-release pressure. Carefully remove lid, allowing steam to escape away from you. Using tongs, transfer clams to bowl, discarding any that have not opened, and cover to keep warm.

4 Stir remaining 2 cups broth, peas, and artichokes into rice and cook, using highest sauté function, until heated through, about 3 minutes. (Mixture will be loose.) Season with salt and pepper to taste. Divide rice mixture between individual serving bowls and top with clams. Serve, passing Salsa Verde separately.

per serving
Cal 600; Total Fat 23g; Sat Fat 3g; Chol 25mg; Sodium 1220mg; Total Carbs 71g, Fiber 5g, Total Sugar 5g; Added Sugar 0g; Protein 26g

mussels with fennel and leeks

serves 4   **total time** 45 minutes

- 1 tablespoon extra-virgin olive oil, plus extra for drizzling

- 1 fennel bulb, 1 tablespoon fronds minced, stalks discarded, bulb halved, cored, and sliced thin

- 1 leek, ends trimmed, leek halved lengthwise, sliced 1 inch thick, and washed thoroughly

- 4 garlic cloves, minced

- 3 sprigs fresh thyme

- ¼ teaspoon red pepper flakes

- ½ cup dry white wine

- 3 pounds mussels, scrubbed and debearded

why this recipe works For such a seemingly simple dish, achieving perfectly cooked mussels can be tricky, with most stove-top recipes inevitably turning out some overcooked and some undercooked mussels. The Instant Pot takes the guesswork out of the process, surrounding them with steam, resulting in a pot full of evenly cooked, plump, tender mussels every time. Anise-forward fennel, leek, garlic, thyme, and red pepper flakes provided a nice base for the mussels, and because the mussels are actually cooking while coming to pressure, we immediately turned off the pot and quick-released the pressure as soon as it reached pressure. Wine, supplemented by the juices released by the mussels and vegetables during cooking, delivered a sauce with balanced flavor and just the right amount of brightness. Discard any raw mussels with an unpleasant odor or with a cracked or broken shell that won't close. To prevent the mussels from overcooking, be sure to turn off the Instant Pot as soon as it reaches pressure. Serve with crusty bread or Garlic Toasts (page 19), if desired.

1 Using highest sauté function, heat oil in Instant Pot until shimmering. Add fennel and leek and cook until softened, about 5 minutes. Stir in garlic, thyme sprigs, and pepper flakes and cook until fragrant, about 30 seconds. Stir in wine, then add mussels.

2 Lock lid in place and close pressure release valve. Select high pressure cook function and set cook time for 0 minutes. Once Instant Pot has reached pressure, immediately turn off pot and quick-release pressure. Carefully remove lid, allowing steam to escape away from you.

3 Discard thyme sprigs and any mussels that have not opened. Transfer mussels to individual serving bowls, sprinkle with fennel fronds, and drizzle with extra oil. Serve.

per serving
Cal 380; Total Fat 11g; Sat Fat 2g; Chol 95mg; Sodium 1010mg; Total Carbs 22g, Fiber 2g, Total Sugar 3g; Added Sugar 0g; Protein 42g

chicken, beef, pork, and lamb

za'atar rubbed chicken with celery root and spinach

serves 4   **total time** 45 minutes

2 (12-ounce) bone-in split chicken breasts, skin removed, trimmed

2 teaspoons za'atar

¾ teaspoon table salt, divided

2 pounds celery root, peeled, halved, and sliced ¾ inch thick

1 tablespoon extra-virgin olive oil

¼ teaspoon pepper

½ cup chicken broth

10 ounces (10 cups) baby spinach

½ teaspoon grated lemon zest

¼ cup pomegranate seeds

3 tablespoons coarsely chopped fresh mint

¼ cup Tahini Sauce (page 18)

why this recipe works Za'atar, a Middle Eastern spice mixture of thyme, sumac, and sesame, makes an easy and impressive rub for chicken. Mild bone-in chicken breasts were the ideal canvas for the spice mixture, and they cooked at the same rate as slightly sweet, starchy celery root. Once the chicken and celery root had finished cooking, we wilted an abundant amount of baby spinach in our braising liquid. Our Tahini Sauce (page 18) not only offered some creaminess, but also echoed the sesame in the za'atar. Fresh mint and pomegranate seeds contributed a final pop of freshness. We prefer to make our own Za'atar (page 19), but any store-bought variety will work.

1 Pat chicken dry with paper towels and sprinkle with za'atar and ½ teaspoon salt. Toss celery root with oil, remaining ¼ teaspoon salt, and pepper in bowl. Add broth to Instant Pot. Place chicken skinned side up in pot, then arrange celery root slabs on top. Lock lid in place and close pressure release valve. Select high pressure cook function and cook for 5 minutes.

2 Turn off Instant Pot and quick-release pressure. Carefully remove lid, allowing steam to escape away from you. Transfer celery root to serving dish and chicken to cutting board. Tent both with aluminum foil and let rest while preparing spinach.

3 Add spinach, 1 handful at a time, to cooking liquid left in pot and cook using highest sauté function until wilted and tender, about 2 minutes. Stir in lemon zest and season with salt and pepper to taste. Using tongs, transfer spinach to serving dish with celery root. Sprinkle with pomegranate seeds and mint. Carve chicken from bones and slice ½ inch thick. Serve with vegetables, passing Tahini Sauce separately.

per serving
Cal 360; Total Fat 11g; Sat Fat 2g; Chol 80mg; Sodium 800mg; Total Carbs 26g, Fiber 7g, Total Sugar 5g; Added Sugar 0g; Protein 32g

greek-style chicken and rice

serves 4   **total time** 1 hour

- 2 (12-ounce) bone-in split chicken breasts, trimmed
- ¾ teaspoon table salt, divided
- ¼ teaspoon pepper
- 1 tablespoon extra-virgin olive oil
- 1 onion, chopped fine
- 2 celery ribs, sliced ¼ inch thick
- 4 garlic cloves, minced
- 2 cups chicken broth
- 1½ cups long-grain white rice, rinsed
- 3 bay leaves
- ¾ cup frozen peas, thawed
- 4 teaspoons capers, rinsed
- 2 tablespoons chopped fresh oregano
- ½ cup Lemon-Yogurt Sauce (page 18)

why this recipe works A steaming bowl of oregano-scented rice studded with sweet peas and briny capers, and served alongside juicy chicken breasts, is our idea of a feel-good meal. Bone-in chicken breasts ensured the meat stayed moist, and browning the breasts before cooking them with the rice added depth to the whole dish. The key to avoiding gluey rice? We simply fluffed the rice with a fork to combine it with peas and capers instead of stirring. A drizzle of our Lemon-Yogurt Sauce (page 18) elevated the meal with bright creaminess and pleasant tang.

1   Pat chicken dry with paper towels and sprinkle with ½ teaspoon salt and pepper. Using highest sauté function, heat oil in Instant Pot for 5 minutes (or until just smoking). Place chicken skin side down in pot and cook until well browned on 1 side, about 5 minutes; transfer to plate.

2   Add onion, celery, and remaining ¼ teaspoon salt to fat left in pot and cook, using highest sauté function, until vegetables are softened, about 5 minutes. Stir in garlic and cook until fragrant, about 30 seconds. Stir in broth, rice, and bay leaves, scraping up any browned bits. Nestle chicken skin side up into rice and add any accumulated juices. Lock lid in place and close pressure release valve. Select high pressure cook function and cook for 4 minutes.

3   Turn off Instant Pot and quick-release pressure. Carefully remove lid, allowing steam to escape away from you. Transfer chicken to cutting board and discard skin, if desired. Tent with aluminum foil and let rest while finishing rice.

4   Discard bay leaves. Add peas and capers and gently fluff rice with fork to combine. Lay clean dish towel over pot, replace lid, and let sit for 5 minutes. Gently fold in oregano. Carve chicken from bones and slice ½ inch thick. Serve with rice and Lemon-Yogurt Sauce.

per serving
Cal 470; Total Fat 8g; Sat Fat 2g; Chol 85mg; Sodium 870mg; Total Carbs 64g, Fiber 2g, Total Sugar 5g; Added Sugar 0g; Protein 35g

chicken and spiced freekeh with cilantro and preserved lemon

serves 4   **total time** 1 hour

- 2 tablespoons extra-virgin olive oil, plus extra for drizzling

- 1 onion, chopped fine

- 4 garlic cloves, minced

- 1½ teaspoons smoked paprika

- ¼ teaspoon ground cardamom

- ¼ teaspoon red pepper flakes

- 2¼ cups chicken broth

- 1½ cups cracked freekeh, rinsed

- 2 (12-ounce) bone-in split chicken breasts, halved crosswise and trimmed

- ½ teaspoon table salt

- ¼ teaspoon pepper

- ¼ cup chopped fresh cilantro

- 2 tablespoons sesame seeds, toasted

- ½ preserved lemon, pulp and white pith removed, rind rinsed and minced (2 tablespoons)

why this recipe works Smoky, earthy freekeh shines in this satisfying one-pot meal. Cooking the grain at the same time as the chicken—and forgoing water, instead using chicken broth bolstered with spices—upped the savoriness, and preserved lemon brought intense brightness. You can find freekeh in the grain aisle or natural foods section of most well-stocked supermarkets; it is sometimes spelled *frikeh* or *farik*. Do not substitute whole freekeh in this dish, as it requires a different cooking method and will not work in this recipe. We think the fragrant and floral notes of preserved lemon are an important addition to this dish, but if you can't find it you can substitute 1 tablespoon lemon zest or use our Quick Preserved Lemon (page 19). Serve with yogurt.

1 Using highest sauté function, heat oil in Instant Pot until shimmering. Add onion and cook until softened, about 5 minutes. Stir in garlic, paprika, cardamom, and pepper flakes and cook until fragrant, about 30 seconds. Stir in broth and freekeh. Sprinkle chicken with salt and pepper. Nestle skin side up into freekeh mixture. Lock lid in place and close pressure release valve. Select high pressure cook function and cook for 5 minutes.

2 Turn off Instant Pot and quick-release pressure. Carefully remove lid, allowing steam to escape away from you. Transfer chicken to serving dish and discard skin, if desired. Tent with aluminum foil and let rest while finishing freekeh.

3 Gently fluff freekeh with fork. Lay clean dish towel over pot, replace lid, and let sit for 5 minutes. Season with salt and pepper to taste. Transfer freekeh to serving dish with chicken and sprinkle with cilantro, sesame seeds, and preserved lemon. Drizzle with extra oil and serve.

per serving
Cal 490; Total Fat 14g; Sat Fat 2g; Chol 80mg; Sodium 980mg; Total Carbs 54g, Fiber 12g, Total Sugar 2g; Added Sugar 0g; Protein 36g

braised chicken with mushrooms and tomatoes

serves 4   **total time** 1 hour

1 tablespoon extra-virgin olive oil

1 pound portobello mushroom caps, gills removed, caps halved and sliced ½ inch thick

1 onion, chopped fine

¾ teaspoon salt, divided

4 garlic cloves, minced

1 tablespoon tomato paste

1 tablespoon all-purpose flour

2 teaspoons minced fresh sage

½ cup dry red wine

1 (14.5-ounce) can diced tomatoes, drained

4 (5- to 7-ounce) bone-in chicken thighs, skin removed, trimmed

¼ teaspoon pepper

2 tablespoons chopped fresh parsley

Shaved Parmesan cheese

why this recipe works We were inspired by *cacciatore*—which means "hunter style" in Italian—a dish known for its rustic ingredients, and traditionally long-simmered and served after a hunt. We wanted dinner on the table in a fraction of the time but without sacrificing any of the flavor. Cooking bone-in chicken thighs in a combination of red wine and diced tomatoes seasoned with fresh sage, yielded moist, well-seasoned chicken. (Removing the skin before cooking prevented the sauce from becoming too oily.) Umami-rich portobello mushrooms and tomato paste heightened the meaty notes. Serve with polenta.

1 Using highest sauté function, heat oil in Instant Pot until shimmering. Add mushrooms, onion, and ¼ teaspoon salt. Partially cover and cook until mushrooms are softened and have released their liquid, about 5 minutes. Stir in garlic, tomato paste, flour, and sage and cook until fragrant, about 1 minute. Stir in wine, scraping up any browned bits, then stir in tomatoes.

2 Sprinkle chicken with remaining ½ teaspoon salt and pepper. Nestle chicken skinned side up into pot and spoon some of sauce on top. Lock lid in place and close pressure release valve. Select high pressure cook function and cook for 15 minutes.

3 Turn off Instant Pot and quick-release pressure. Carefully remove lid, allowing steam to escape away from you. Transfer chicken to serving dish, tent with aluminum foil, and let rest while finishing sauce.

4 Using highest sauté function, bring sauce to simmer and cook until thickened slightly, about 5 minutes. Season sauce with salt and pepper to taste. Spoon sauce over chicken and sprinkle with parsley and Parmesan. Serve.

per serving
Cal 230; Total Fat 7g; Sat Fat 1.5g; Chol 80mg; Sodium 730mg; Total Carbs 15g, Fiber 2g, Total Sugar 6g; Added Sugar 0g; Protein 21g

chicken tagine

serves 4   **total time** 1 hour

2 (15-ounce) cans chickpeas, rinsed, divided

1 tablespoon extra-virgin olive oil

5 garlic cloves, minced

1½ teaspoons paprika

½ teaspoon ground turmeric

½ teaspoon ground cumin

¼ teaspoon ground ginger

¼ teaspoon cayenne pepper

1 fennel bulb, 1 tablespoon fronds minced, stalks discarded, bulb halved and cut lengthwise into ½-inch-thick wedges

1 cup chicken broth

3 (2-inch) strips lemon zest, plus lemon wedges for serving

4 (5- to 7-ounce) bone-in chicken thighs, skin removed, trimmed

½ teaspoon table salt

½ cup pitted large brine-cured green or black olives, halved

⅓ cup raisins

2 tablespoons chopped fresh parsley

why this recipe works This cornerstone of Moroccan cuisine, heady with spices, salty with olives, and bright with lemon, is a balancing act of flavors ready-made for the Instant Pot—the enclosed environment ensures none of that flavor escapes. We loved our Fish Tagine (page 107) and wanted the same assertive, intensely spiced stew in a heartier application. For the chicken, we used thighs instead of breasts for deep intensity. Fresh fennel and readily available canned chickpeas (some of them mashed into a paste to thicken the tagine) gave our meal heft. Next we tackled the defining spices: Paprika, cumin, and ginger lent depth and a little sweetness, cayenne added subtle heat, and aromatic turmeric colored the broth a deep, attractive yellow. Raisins lent a pleasant floral flavor, as did a couple of wide strips of lemon zest. Brine-cured olives provided a salty counterpart to the sweet and complex broth. Don't core the fennel before cutting it into wedges; the core helps hold the wedges together during cooking.

1 Using potato masher, mash ½ cup chickpeas in bowl to paste. Using highest sauté function, cook oil, garlic, paprika, turmeric, cumin, ginger, and cayenne in Instant Pot until fragrant, about 1 minute. Turn off Instant Pot, then stir in remaining whole chickpeas, mashed chickpeas, fennel wedges, broth, and zest.

2 Sprinkle chicken with salt. Nestle chicken skinned side up into pot and spoon some of cooking liquid over top. Lock lid in place and close pressure release valve. Select high pressure cook function and cook for 10 minutes.

3 Turn off Instant Pot and quick-release pressure. Carefully remove lid, allowing steam to escape away from you. Discard lemon zest. Stir in olives, raisins, parsley, and fennel fronds. Season with salt and pepper to taste. Serve with lemon wedges.

per serving
Cal 340; Total Fat 11g; Sat Fat 2g; Chol 80mg; Sodium 1000mg; Total Carbs 35g, Fiber 9g, Total Sugar 11g; Added Sugar 0g; Protein 25g

lemony chicken with fingerling potatoes and olives

serves 4   total time 1 hour

- 4 (5- to 7-ounce) bone-in chicken thighs, trimmed
- ½ teaspoon table salt
- ¼ teaspoon pepper
- 2 teaspoons extra-virgin olive oil, plus extra for drizzling
- 4 garlic cloves, peeled and smashed
- ½ cup chicken broth
- 1 small lemon, sliced thin
- 1½ pounds fingerling potatoes, unpeeled
- ¼ cup pitted brine-cured green or black olives, halved
- 2 tablespoons coarsely chopped fresh parsley

why this recipe works In this simple dish, tender, juicy chicken thighs and delicate fingerling potatoes absorb the bright aromas of a classic Provençal combination: garlic, lemon, and olives. We started by browning the chicken thighs in olive oil. We then briefly set aside the browned chicken so we could toast garlic cloves and add chicken broth and a whole sliced lemon to create a vibrant cooking liquid. We returned the chicken to the pot and added the potatoes, and cooked it all under pressure. We especially loved the brightness and supple texture of the braised lemon slices. Olives, fresh parsley, and a drizzle of olive oil were the perfect finish. Use potatoes that are approximately 1 inch in diameter. Slice the lemon as thinly as possible; this allows them to melt into the sauce.

1   Pat chicken dry with paper towels and sprinkle with salt and pepper. Using highest sauté function, heat oil in Instant Pot for 5 minutes (or until just smoking). Place chicken skin side down in pot and cook until well browned on first side, about 5 minutes; transfer to plate.

2   Add garlic to fat left in pot and cook, using highest sauté function, until golden and fragrant, about 2 minutes. Stir in broth and lemon, scraping up any browned bits. Return chicken skin side up to pot and add any accumulated juices. Arrange potatoes on top. Lock lid in place and close pressure release valve. Select high pressure cook function and cook for 9 minutes.

3   Turn off Instant Pot and quick-release pressure. Carefully remove lid, allowing steam to escape away from you. Transfer chicken to serving dish and discard skin, if desired. Stir olives and parsley into potatoes and season with salt and pepper to taste. Serve chicken with potatoes.

per serving
Cal 280; Total Fat 7g; Sat Fat 1.5g; Chol 80mg; Sodium 580mg; Total Carbs 33g, Fiber 4g, Total Sugar 1g; Added Sugar 0g; Protein 20g

chicken with lentils and butternut squash

serves 4 **total time** 1 hour 15 minutes

- 2 large shallots, halved and sliced thin, divided
- 5 teaspoons extra-virgin olive oil, divided
- ½ teaspoon grated lemon zest plus 2 teaspoons juice
- 1 teaspoon table salt, divided
- 4 (5- to 7-ounce) bone-in chicken thighs, trimmed
- ¼ teaspoon pepper
- 2 garlic cloves, minced
- 1½ teaspoons caraway seeds
- 1 teaspoon ground coriander
- 1 teaspoon ground cumin
- ½ teaspoon paprika
- ⅛ teaspoon cayenne pepper
- 2 cups chicken broth
- 1 cup French green lentils, picked over and rinsed
- 2 pounds butternut squash, peeled, seeded, and cut into 1½-inch pieces (6 cups)
- 1 cup fresh parsley or cilantro leaves

why this recipe works Rich, tender chicken with stewed lentils and butternut squash is classic North African fare. We bloomed a mixture of warm, floral spices to infuse the lentils as they cooked. We then stirred in the lentils, broth, and butternut squash, and nestled the chicken on top before cooking everything under pressure until the squash softened and melted into the lentils, its sweetness tempering the vegetal legumes. We made a quick salad from parsley (or cilantro) leaves and shallot, with a lemon vinaigrette as the dressing. The brightness from the leafy green herbs and the subtle sharpness from the shallot tied the whole dish together and provided a nice contrast to the braised earthiness of the lentils. We prefer French green lentils, or *lentilles du Puy*, for this recipe, but it will work with any type of lentil except red or yellow.

1 Combine half of shallots, 1 tablespoon oil, lemon zest and juice, and ¼ teaspoon salt in bowl; set aside. Pat chicken dry with paper towels and sprinkle with ½ teaspoon salt and pepper. Using highest sauté function, heat remaining 2 teaspoons oil in Instant Pot for 5 minutes (or until just smoking). Place chicken skin side down in pot and cook until well browned on first side, about 5 minutes; transfer to plate.

2 Add remaining shallot and remaining ¼ teaspoon salt to fat left in pot and cook, using highest sauté function, until shallot is softened, about 2 minutes. Stir in garlic, caraway, coriander, cumin, paprika, and cayenne and cook until fragrant, about 30 seconds. Stir in broth, scraping up any browned bits, then stir in lentils.

3 Nestle chicken skin side up into lentils and add any accumulated juices. Arrange squash on top. Lock lid in place and close pressure release valve. Select high pressure cook function and cook for 15 minutes.

4 Turn off Instant Pot and quick-release pressure. Carefully remove lid, allowing steam to escape away from you. Transfer chicken to plate and discard skin, if desired. Season lentil mixture with salt and pepper to taste. Add parsley to shallot mixture and toss to combine. Serve chicken with lentil mixture, topping individual portions with shallot-parsley salad.

per serving
Cal 430; Total Fat 11g; Sat Fat 2g; Chol 80mg; Sodium 970mg; Total Carbs 55g, Fiber 13g, Total Sugar 7g; Added Sugar 0g; Protein 30g

braised short ribs with fennel and pickled grapes

serves 4   **total time** 1 hour 45 minutes

1½ pounds boneless beef short ribs, trimmed and cut into 2-inch pieces

1 teaspoon table salt, divided

1 tablespoon extra-virgin olive oil

1 fennel bulb, 2 tablespoons fronds chopped, stalks discarded, bulb halved, cored, and sliced into 1-inch-thick wedges

1 onion, halved and sliced ½ inch thick

4 garlic cloves, minced

2 teaspoons fennel seeds

½ cup chicken broth

1 sprig fresh rosemary

¼ cup red wine vinegar

1 tablespoon sugar

4 ounces seedless red grapes, halved (½ cup)

why this recipe works This dish is evocative of southern Italy after a grape harvest, combining boneless beef short ribs with aromatic fennel, plus the unique sweet-tart punch of quick-pickled grapes. We started by browning our short ribs in the Instant Pot, and then we built an aromatic broth using fennel, onion, garlic, fennel seeds, and rosemary. We cooked everything under pressure for 35 minutes, which resulted in short ribs that were fall-apart tender. We strained the vegetables and then defatted the braising liquid, pouring a measured amount of the liquid over the beef and vegetables. The thickness and marbling of boneless short ribs can vary a good deal. Look for lean ribs cut from the chuck that are approximately 1½ to 2 inches thick and 4 to 5 inches long. If boneless short ribs are unavailable, you can substitute an equal amount of boneless beef chuck-eye roast. Don't core the fennel before cutting it into wedges; the core helps hold the wedges together during cooking.

1 Pat short ribs dry with paper towels and sprinkle with ½ teaspoon salt. Using highest sauté function, heat oil in Instant Pot for 5 minutes (or until just smoking). Brown short ribs on all sides, 6 to 8 minutes; transfer to plate.

2 Add fennel wedges, onion, and ¼ teaspoon salt to fat left in pot and cook, using highest sauté function, until vegetables are softened and lightly browned, about 5 minutes. Stir in garlic and fennel seeds and cook until fragrant, about 30 seconds. Stir in broth and rosemary sprig, scraping up any browned bits. Nestle short ribs into vegetable mixture and add any accumulated juices. Lock lid in place and close pressure release valve. Select high pressure cook function and cook for 35 minutes.

3 Meanwhile, microwave vinegar, sugar, and remaining ¼ teaspoon salt in bowl until simmering, about 1 minute. Add grapes and let sit, stirring occasionally, for 20 minutes. Drain grapes and return to now-empty bowl. (Drained grapes can be refrigerated for up to 1 week.)

4 Turn off Instant Pot and let pressure release naturally for 15 minutes. Quick-release any remaining pressure, then carefully remove lid, allowing steam to escape away from you. Transfer short ribs to serving dish, tent with aluminum foil, and let rest while finishing sauce.

5 Strain braising liquid through fine-mesh strainer into fat separator. Discard rosemary sprig and transfer vegetables to serving dish with beef. Let braising liquid settle for 5 minutes, then pour ¾ cup defatted liquid over short ribs and vegetables; discard remaining liquid. Sprinkle with grapes and fennel fronds. Serve.

per serving
Cal 310; Total Fat 17g; Sat Fat 6g; Chol 70mg; Sodium 750mg; Total Carbs 15g, Fiber 3g, Total Sugar 10g; Added Sugar 1g; Protein 24g

wine-braised short ribs with potatoes

serves 4   **total time** 2 hours 15 minutes

2 pounds bone-in English-style beef short ribs, trimmed

¾ teaspoon table salt, divided

¼ teaspoon pepper

1 tablespoon extra-virgin olive oil

1 onion, chopped fine

6 garlic cloves, minced

2 tablespoons tomato paste

1 tablespoon minced fresh oregano or 1 teaspoon dried

1 (14.5-ounce) can whole peeled tomatoes, drained with ¼ cup juice reserved, chopped coarse

½ cup dry red wine

1 pound small red potatoes, unpeeled, halved

2 tablespoons minced fresh parsley

why this recipe works This elegant meal is perfect for a dinner party but easy enough to make almost anytime. Bone-in beef short ribs are cooked under pressure to tender perfection and served with red potatoes in a smoothly acidic, complex sauce. We started by browning the short ribs to create a flavorful base for the braising liquid. To the fond in the pot we added onion, garlic, oregano, red wine, whole peeled tomatoes, and a bit of tomato paste. After 60 minutes under pressure, the short ribs were perfectly cooked. As the ribs rested, we defatted the braising liquid, and then used it to cook our potatoes in just 4 minutes under pressure. A sprinkle of fresh parsley was the perfect finish. English-style short ribs contain a single rib bone; choose ribs that are 4 to 6 inches in length and have at least 1 inch of meat on top of the bone. Use small red potatoes measuring 1 to 2 inches in diameter.

1   Pat short ribs dry with paper towels and sprinkle with ½ teaspoon salt and pepper. Using highest sauté function, heat oil in Instant Pot for 5 minutes (or until just smoking). Brown short ribs on all sides, 6 to 8 minutes; transfer to plate.

2   Add onion and remaining ¼ teaspoon salt to fat left in pot and cook, using highest sauté function, until onion is softened, about 3 minutes. Stir in garlic, tomato paste, and oregano and cook until fragrant, about 30 seconds. Stir in tomatoes and reserved juice and wine, scraping up any browned bits. Nestle short ribs meat side down into pot and add any accumulated juices. Lock lid in place and close pressure release valve. Select high pressure cook function and cook for 60 minutes.

3   Turn off Instant Pot and let pressure release naturally for 15 minutes. Quick-release any remaining pressure, then carefully remove lid, allowing steam to escape away from you. Transfer short ribs to serving dish, tent with aluminum foil, and let rest while preparing potatoes.

4 Strain braising liquid through fine-mesh strainer into fat separator; transfer solids to now-empty pot. Let braising liquid settle for 5 minutes, then pour 1½ cups defatted liquid and any accumulated juices into pot with solids; discard remaining liquid. Add potatoes. Lock lid in place and close pressure release valve. Select high pressure cook function and cook for 4 minutes.

Turn off Instant Pot and quick-release pressure. Carefully remove lid, allowing steam to escape away from you.

5 Using slotted spoon, transfer potatoes to serving dish. Season sauce with salt and pepper to taste. Spoon sauce over short ribs and potatoes and sprinkle with parsley. Serve.

per serving
Cal 340; Total Fat 13g; Sat Fat 4.5g; Chol 55mg; Sodium 700mg; Total Carbs 29g, Fiber 3g, Total Sugar 7g; Added Sugar 0g; Protein 21g

chicken, beef, pork, and lamb   135

smothered pork chops with leeks and mustard

serves 4   **total time** 1 hour 30 minutes

- 4 (8- to 10-ounce) bone-in blade-cut pork chops, about ¾ inch thick, trimmed
- ½ teaspoon table salt
- ½ teaspoon pepper
- 4 teaspoons extra-virgin olive oil, divided
- 2 ounces pancetta, chopped fine
- 1 tablespoon all-purpose flour
- ¾ cup dry white wine
- 1½ pounds leeks, ends trimmed, halved lengthwise, sliced into 3-inch lengths, and washed thoroughly
- 1 tablespoon Dijon mustard
- 2 tablespoons chopped fresh parsley

why this recipe works This dish takes its cue from the classic Provençal combination of sweet, aromatic leeks and bright, tangy Dijon mustard. The Instant Pot transforms a hefty pound and a half of leeks (including their usually tough dark green parts) into a luscious, pungent, meltingly tender topping for our flavorful pork chops in the same amount of time it took to cook the chops. Blade chops—with their combination of light and dark meat, connective tissue, marbled fat, and bone—were perfect for pressure cooking since the meat stayed tender and moist, and the other elements (like salty, meaty pancetta) gave great flavor and texture to the sauce. To keep the chops from buckling during cooking, we simply snipped through the fat surrounding the loin muscle of each chop to release the tension. Look for blade chops that are about ¾ inches thick.

1   Pat pork chops dry with paper towels. Using sharp knife, cut 2 slits, about 2 inches apart, through fat on edge of each chop. Sprinkle with salt and pepper. Using highest sauté function, heat 2 teaspoons oil in Instant Pot for 5 minutes (or until just smoking). Brown 2 chops on both sides, 6 to 8 minutes; transfer to plate. Repeat with remaining 2 teaspoons oil and remaining chops; transfer to plate.

2   Add pancetta to fat left in pot and cook, using highest sauté function, until softened and lightly browned, about 2 minutes. Stir in flour and cook for 30 seconds. Stir in wine, scraping up any browned bits and smoothing any lumps. Stir in leeks and cook until softened, about 3 minutes. Nestle chops into pot (chops will overlap) and add any accumulated juices. Lock lid in place and close pressure release valve. Select high pressure cook function and cook for 10 minutes.

3 Turn off Instant Pot and let pressure release naturally for 15 minutes. Quick-release any remaining pressure, then carefully remove lid, allowing steam to escape away from you. Transfer chops to serving platter, tent with aluminum foil, and let rest while finishing leeks.

4 Using highest sauté function, bring leek mixture to simmer. Stir in mustard and cook until slightly thickened, about 5 minutes. Season with salt and pepper to taste. Spoon leek mixture over chops and sprinkle with parsley. Serve.

per serving
Cal 390; Total Fat 17g; Sat Fat 5g; Chol 95mg; Sodium 780mg; Total Carbs 13g, Fiber 1g, Total Sugar 3g; Added Sugar 0g; Protein 35g

braised pork with broccoli rabe and sage

serves 4 **total time** 1 hour 15 minutes

1½ pounds boneless pork butt roast, trimmed and cut into 2-inch pieces

½ teaspoon table salt

½ teaspoon pepper

1 tablespoon extra-virgin olive oil

2 tablespoons minced fresh sage, divided

5 garlic cloves, peeled and smashed

1 tablespoon all-purpose flour

¼ cup chicken broth

¼ cup dry white wine

1 pound broccoli rabe, trimmed and cut into 1-inch pieces

½ teaspoon grated orange zest

why this recipe works This recipe is far greater than the sum of its simple parts: Tender, meaty pork and deliciously bitter broccoli rabe are joined in a silky, aromatic sauce. We started by browning pieces of juicy, richly flavored pork butt, then combined garlic, white wine, and aromatic sage with the fond in the pot (with just a touch of flour to add body) to build the braising liquid. After releasing the pressure, we removed the tender pork. As it rested, we cooked the broccoli rabe in the remaining sauce for just 3 minutes using the sauté function. A half teaspoon of freshly grated orange zest added a final burst of brightness. Pork butt roast is often labeled Boston butt in the supermarket.

1 Pat pork dry with paper towels and sprinkle with salt and pepper. Using highest sauté function, heat oil in Instant Pot for 5 minutes (or until just smoking). Brown pork on all sides, 6 to 8 minutes; transfer to plate.

2 Add 1 tablespoon sage, garlic, and flour to fat left in pot and cook, using highest sauté function, until fragrant, about 1 minute. Stir in broth and wine, scraping up any browned bits. Return pork to pot along with any accumulated juices. Lock lid in place and close pressure release valve. Select high pressure cook function and cook for 30 minutes.

3 Turn off Instant Pot and let pressure release naturally for 15 minutes. Quick-release any remaining pressure, then carefully remove lid, allowing steam to escape away from you. Transfer pork to serving dish, tent with aluminum foil, and let rest while preparing broccoli rabe.

4 Whisk sauce until smooth and bring to simmer using highest sauté function. Stir in broccoli rabe and cook, partially covered, until tender and bright green, about 3 minutes. Stir in orange zest and remaining 1 tablespoon sage. Serve pork with broccoli rabe mixture.

per serving
Cal 340; Total Fat 16g; Sat Fat 5g; Chol 115mg; Sodium 490mg; Total Carbs 7g, Fiber 3g, Total Sugar 1g; Added Sugar 0g; Protein 37g

pork sausage with white beans and mustard greens

serves 4   **total time** 1 hour

- 2 tablespoons extra-virgin olive oil, divided
- 1 pound hot or sweet Italian sausage (4 sausages)
- 1 onion, chopped fine
- 1 tablespoon minced fresh thyme or 1 teaspoon dried
- 2 garlic cloves, minced
- ¾ cup chicken broth
- ¼ cup dry white wine
- 2 (15-ounce) cans navy beans, rinsed
- 1 pound mustard greens, stemmed and cut into 2-inch pieces
- ½ cup panko bread crumbs
- 2 tablespoons chopped fresh parsley
- ½ teaspoon grated lemon zest plus 1 teaspoon juice
- 4 ounces goat cheese, crumbled (1 cup)

why this recipe works The south of France is known for its rich stews that combine meaty sausage, creamy white beans, and fresh greens. For our slightly less stew-y version, we first browned easy-to-find Italian sausage and then pressure-cooked it with convenient canned navy beans and peppery mustard greens. For a bright, textural finish, we made lemon-scented bread crumbs to sprinkle over the completed dish along with tangy goat cheese. If mustard greens are unavailable, you can substitute kale.

1 Using highest sauté function, heat 1 tablespoon oil in Instant Pot for 5 minutes (or until just smoking). Brown sausages on all sides, 6 to 8 minutes; transfer to plate.

2 Add onion to fat left in pot and cook, using highest sauté function, until softened, about 5 minutes. Stir in thyme and garlic and cook until fragrant, about 30 seconds. Stir in broth and wine, scraping up any browned bits, then stir in beans. Add mustard greens, then place sausages on top. Lock lid in place and close pressure release valve. Select high pressure cook function and cook for 2 minutes.

3 Meanwhile, toss panko with remaining 1 tablespoon oil in bowl until evenly coated. Microwave, stirring every 30 seconds, until light golden brown, about 5 minutes. Let cool slightly, then stir in parsley and lemon zest; set aside for serving.

4 Turn off Instant Pot and quick-release pressure. Carefully remove lid, allowing steam to escape away from you. Transfer sausages to plate. Stir lemon juice into bean and mustard greens mixture and season with salt and pepper to taste. Serve sausages with bean and mustard green mixture, sprinkling individual portions with seasoned bread crumbs and goat cheese.

per serving
Cal 520; Total Fat 23g; Sat Fat 9g; Chol 45mg; Sodium 1280mg; Total Carbs 41g, Fiber 11g, Total Sugar 5g; Added Sugar 0g; Protein 38g

lamb meatballs with couscous, pickled onions, and tahini

serves 4   **total time** 1 hour

½ cup Tahini Sauce (page 18), divided

3 tablespoons panko bread crumbs

1 pound ground lamb

¼ cup chopped fresh mint, divided

1 teaspoon ground cinnamon, divided

1 teaspoon ground cumin, divided

¾ teaspoon table salt, divided

1 tablespoon extra-virgin olive oil

1 onion, chopped fine

⅛ teaspoon cayenne pepper

1 cup chicken broth, plus extra as needed

1 cup couscous

½ cup jarred roasted red peppers, rinsed, patted dry, and chopped

1 teaspoon grated lemon zest plus 1 tablespoon juice

⅓ cup Quick Pickled Onions (page 19)

why this recipe works Tahini, a potent paste made from toasted sesame seeds, has a texture similar to natural peanut butter. Apart from its being a core ingredient in hummus, we love it in our drizzle-friendly Tahini Sauce (page 18). We wanted this sauce to take center stage, so we made it do double duty by mixing it with bread crumbs as a riff on a panade (typically made from bread pieces soaked and mashed in milk or yogurt and then mixed into meatballs to keep them moist) and also spooning it over the finished meatballs on a bed of warmly spiced couscous with roasted red peppers and pickled onions. Lamb's robust grassy flavor was a perfect companion to tahini's smooth nuttiness. The meatballs cooked in just 1 minute under pressure, and as they rested separately, we simply stirred the couscous into the remaining liquid and allowed it to cook in the residual heat and absorb the bold and delicious flavors. You can substitute an equal amount of 85 percent lean ground beef for the lamb, if desired.

1   Using fork, mash ¼ cup Tahini Sauce and panko together in bowl to form paste. Add ground lamb, 2 tablespoons mint, ½ teaspoon cinnamon, ½ teaspoon cumin, and ½ teaspoon salt, and knead with hands until thoroughly combined. Pinch off and roll mixture into twelve 1½-inch meatballs.

2   Using highest sauté function, heat oil in Instant Pot until shimmering. Add onion and remaining ¼ teaspoon salt and cook until onion is softened, about 5 minutes. Stir in remaining ½ teaspoon cinnamon, remaining ½ teaspoon cumin, and cayenne and cook until fragrant, about 30 seconds. Stir in broth, scraping up any browned bits. Add meatballs to pot. Lock lid in place and close pressure release valve. Select high pressure cook function and cook for 1 minute.

3 Turn off Instant Pot and quick-release pressure. Carefully remove lid, allowing steam to escape away from you. Using slotted spoon, transfer meatballs to plate, tent with aluminum foil, and let rest while cooking couscous. (You should have about 2 cups cooking liquid remaining in pot; add extra broth as needed to equal 2 cups.)

4 Using highest sauté function, bring liquid in pot to simmer. Stir in couscous, red peppers, and lemon zest and juice. Turn off Instant Pot, cover, and let sit for 10 minutes. Fluff couscous gently with fork and transfer to serving dish. Arrange meatballs on top and drizzle with remaining ¼ cup Tahini Sauce. Sprinkle with pickled onions and remaining 2 tablespoons mint. Serve.

per serving
Cal 650; Total Fat 36g; Sat Fat 13g; Chol 85mg; Sodium 820mg; Total Carbs 53g, Fiber 4g, Total Sugar 10g; Added Sugar 6g; Protein 29g

lamb chops with shaved zucchini salad

serves 4   **total time** 1 hour 30 minutes

4 (8- to 12-ounce) lamb shoulder chops (blade or round bone), about ¾ inch thick, trimmed

¾ teaspoon table salt, divided

¾ teaspoon pepper, divided

2 tablespoons extra-virgin olive oil, divided

1 onion, chopped

5 garlic cloves, minced

½ cup chicken broth

1 bay leaf

4 zucchini (6 ounces each), sliced lengthwise into ribbons

1 teaspoon grated lemon zest plus 1 tablespoon juice

2 ounces goat cheese, crumbled (½ cup)

¼ cup chopped fresh mint

2 tablespoons raisins

why this recipe works When buying lamb chops, many people turn to the tried-and-true (and expensive) rib or loin chop. The oddly shaped, more affordable shoulder chops rarely get a second look, but their abundance of connective tissue and bone (read: flavor) make them ideal for braising. In just 20 minutes under pressure in the Instant Pot, these economical chops transformed into the fork-tender, juicy focal point of an easy and impressive meal. Rather than combining the lamb with a braised vegetable or grain, we opted for a salad that proved a perfect contrast to the richness of the chops. Tender shaved zucchini with a bright lemony dressing, tangy goat cheese, sweet raisins, and aromatic fresh mint was the perfect accompaniment. The success of the salad depends on using small, in-season zucchini and good olive oil. A vegetable peeler makes easy work of slicing the zucchini into ribbons.

1 Pat lamb chops dry with paper towels and sprinkle with ½ teaspoon salt and ½ teaspoon pepper. Using highest sauté function, heat 1½ teaspoons oil in Instant Pot for 5 minutes (or until just smoking). Brown half of chops on both sides, 6 to 8 minutes; transfer to plate. Repeat with 1½ teaspoons oil and remaining chops; transfer to plate.

2 Add onion to fat left in pot and cook, using highest sauté function, until softened, about 5 minutes. Stir in garlic and cook until fragrant, about 30 seconds. Stir in broth and bay leaf, scraping up any browned bits. Return chops to pot along with any accumulated juices (chops will overlap). Lock lid in place and close pressure release valve. Select high pressure cook function and cook for 20 minutes.

3 Turn off Instant Pot and let pressure release naturally for 15 minutes. Quick-release any remaining pressure, then carefully remove lid, allowing steam to escape away from you. Transfer chops to serving dish. Gently toss zucchini with lemon zest and juice, remaining 1 tablespoon oil, remaining ¼ teaspoon salt, and remaining ¼ teaspoon pepper in bowl. Arrange zucchini on serving dish with lamb, and sprinkle with goat cheese, mint, and raisins. Serve.

per serving
Cal 390; Total Fat 20g; Sat Fat 7g; Chol 110mg; Sodium 720mg; Total Carbs 14g, Fiber 2g, Total Sugar 9g; Added Sugar 0g; Protein 38g

braised lamb shanks with bell pepper and harissa

serves 4   **total time** 2 hours 30 minutes

- 4 (10- to 12-ounce) lamb shanks, trimmed
- ¾ teaspoon salt, divided
- 1 tablespoon extra-virgin olive oil
- 1 onion, chopped
- 1 red bell pepper, stemmed, seeded, and cut into 1-inch pieces
- ¼ cup harissa, divided
- 4 garlic cloves, minced
- 1 tablespoon tomato paste
- ½ cup chicken broth
- 1 bay leaf
- 2 tablespoons chopped fresh mint

why this recipe works Intensely flavorful, meltingly tender lamb shanks are an easy win in the Instant Pot; as with other tougher cuts of meat, what normally takes several hours to braise is ready in just an hour under pressure. But what gives this dish its unique character is the sauce, made from a combination of bell pepper and the Tunisian condiment harissa—a blend of ground chiles, garlic, and spices. To keep our sauce clean and light, we strained and defatted the cooking liquid after braising. We blended the braised bell pepper and onion into a portion of the cooking liquid to create a rich sauce, and sprinkled fresh mint for a sweet finish. We prefer to use our Harissa (page 17), but you can substitute store-bought harissa if you wish, though spiciness can vary greatly by brand. Serve with couscous.

1   Pat lamb shanks dry with paper towels and sprinkle with ½ teaspoon salt. Using highest sauté function, heat oil in Instant Pot for 5 minutes (or until just smoking). Brown 2 shanks on all sides, 8 to 10 minutes; transfer to plate. Repeat with remaining shanks; transfer to plate.

2   Add onion, bell pepper, and remaining ¼ teaspoon salt to fat left in pot and cook, using highest sauté function, until vegetables are softened, about 5 minutes. Stir in 2 tablespoons harissa, garlic, and tomato paste and cook until fragrant, about 30 seconds. Stir in broth and bay leaf, scraping up any browned bits. Nestle shanks into pot and add any accumulated juices. Lock lid in place and close pressure release valve. Select high pressure cook function and cook for 60 minutes.

3   Turn off Instant Pot and let pressure release naturally for 15 minutes. Quick-release any remaining pressure, then carefully remove lid, allowing steam to escape away from you. Transfer shanks to serving dish, tent with aluminum foil, and let rest while finishing sauce.

4 Strain braising liquid through fine-mesh strainer into fat separator. Discard bay leaf and transfer solids to blender. Let braising liquid settle for 5 minutes, then pour ¾ cup defatted liquid into blender with solids; discard remaining liquid.

Add remaining 2 tablespoons harissa and process until smooth, about 1 minute. Season with salt and pepper to taste. Pour portion of sauce over shanks and sprinkle with mint. Serve, passing remaining sauce separately.

per serving
Cal 450; Total Fat 33g; Sat Fat 10g; Chol 100mg; Sodium 780mg; Total Carbs 9g, Fiber 3g, Total Sugar 3g; Added Sugar 0g; Protein 28g

chicken, beef, pork, and lamb   147

vegetable mains

beet and watercress salad with orange and dill

serves 4   **total time** 35 minutes

2 pounds beets, scrubbed, trimmed, and cut into ¾-inch pieces

½ cup water

1 teaspoon caraway seeds

½ teaspoon table salt

1 cup plain Greek yogurt

1 small garlic clove, minced to paste

5 ounces (5 cups) watercress, torn into bite-size pieces

1 tablespoon extra-virgin olive oil, divided, plus extra for drizzling

1 tablespoon white wine vinegar, divided

1 teaspoon grated orange zest plus 2 tablespoons juice

¼ cup hazelnuts, toasted, skinned, and chopped

¼ cup coarsely chopped fresh dill

Coarse sea salt

why this recipe works Sweet, slightly earthy beets do double duty in this refreshing salad bursting with an unexpected combination of ingredients. After quickly cooking the unpeeled beets under pressure with caraway seeds and water (the intense heat of the Instant Pot made the skins undetectable), we stirred the potent cooking liquid into some creamy Greek yogurt, turning it a spectacular pink, perfect as a base for some peppery watercress. Orange zest brightened up the beets, and we arranged them on top of the greens. A sprinkling of dill brought out the anise notes of the caraway seeds, and hazelnuts and coarse sea salt added rich crunchiness. To make this a heartier meal, add Hard- or Soft-Cooked Eggs (page 10) and serve with crusty bread.

1 Combine beets, water, caraway seeds, and table salt in Instant Pot. Lock lid in place and close pressure release valve. Select high pressure cook function and cook for 8 minutes. Turn off Instant Pot and quick-release pressure. Carefully remove lid, allowing steam to escape away from you.

2 Using slotted spoon, transfer beets to plate; set aside to cool slightly. Combine yogurt, garlic, and 3 tablespoons beet cooking liquid in bowl; discard remaining cooking liquid. In large bowl toss watercress with 2 teaspoons oil and 1 teaspoon vinegar. Season with table salt and pepper to taste.

3 Spread yogurt mixture over surface of serving dish. Arrange watercress on top of yogurt mixture, leaving 1-inch border of yogurt mixture. Add beets to now-empty large bowl and toss with orange zest and juice, remaining 2 teaspoons vinegar, and remaining 1 teaspoon oil. Season with table salt and pepper to taste. Arrange beets on top of watercress mixture. Drizzle with extra oil and sprinkle with hazelnuts, dill, and sea salt. Serve.

per serving
Cal 240; Total Fat 15g; Sat Fat 6g; Chol 10mg; Sodium 440mg; Total Carbs 19g, Fiber 5g, Total Sugar 13g; Added Sugar 0g; Protein 9g

meze plate with hummus, spiced carrots, and arugula

serves 4 **total time** 40 minutes

2 pounds carrots, peeled

½ cup chicken or vegetable broth

3 tablespoons Harissa (page 17), divided

½ teaspoon table salt

2 ounces (2 cups) baby arugula

1 tablespoon extra-virgin olive oil

2 teaspoons lemon juice

1½ cups Hummus (page 13)

½ cup Quick Pickled Onions (page 19)

2 tablespoons roasted pepitas

why this recipe works We raided our DIY Mediterranean Pantry (pages 12–19) for this meze-inspired meal, using spicy Harissa (page 17) both for flavoring the liquid in which we cooked our carrots and as a finishing drizzle. To make sure the carrots cooked evenly, we cut them into 3-inch lengths and then halved the thicker pieces lengthwise so that they all were of similar size. Our smooth Hummus (page 13) was the perfect base for our spiced carrots and lightly dressed arugula, Quick Pickled Onions (page 19) brought bright color and acidity, and pepitas added a pleasing crunch. We like to use our homemade Harissa, but you can substitute store-bought harissa, though spiciness among different brands can vary greatly. Our simple homemade Hummus really makes a difference here; however, 1½ cups of any store-bought variety will work. Serve with pita.

1 Cut carrots into 3-inch lengths. Leave thin pieces whole and halve larger pieces lengthwise. Combine carrots, broth, 1 tablespoon Harissa, and salt in Instant Pot. Lock lid in place and close pressure release valve. Select high pressure cook function and cook for 1 minute. Turn off Instant Pot and quick-release pressure. Carefully remove lid, allowing steam to escape away from you; drain carrots.

2 Gently toss arugula with oil and lemon juice in bowl. Season with salt and pepper to taste. Spread portion of Hummus over bottom of individual serving plates. Using slotted spoon, arrange carrots on top and drizzle with remaining 2 tablespoons Harissa. Top with arugula, pickled onions, and pepitas. Serve.

per serving
Cal 560; Total Fat 34g; Sat Fat 4.5g; Chol 0mg; Sodium 1050mg; Total Carbs 66g, Fiber 10g, Total Sugar 17g; Added Sugar 4g; Protein 18g

rustic garlic toasts with stewed tomatoes, shaved fennel, and burrata

serves 4   **total time** 45 minutes

- 2 tablespoons extra-virgin olive oil, divided, plus extra for drizzling

- 5 garlic cloves, sliced thin

- 1½ teaspoons fennel seeds, lightly cracked

- 1 (28-ounce) can whole peeled tomatoes, drained with juice reserved, halved

- ⅛ teaspoon table salt

- 8 ounces burrata cheese, room temperature

- 1 fennel bulb, stalks discarded, bulb halved, cored, and sliced thin

- 4 ounces (4 cups) baby arugula

- 1 recipe Garlic Toasts (page 19)

  Balsamic glaze

  Coarse sea salt

why this recipe works Burrata is a decadent version of mozzarella in which the supple cheese is bound around a filling of cream and soft, stringy curds. It is commonly served with tomatoes, whose natural acidity tempers the richness of the cheese. Cooking whole peeled tomatoes in the Instant Pot turned them tender but not mushy, and their freshness almost intensified under pressure. We spooned them over our Garlic Toasts (page 19), and added a salad of arugula and fresh fennel. The burrata was the final step, drizzled with a sweet-sour balsamic glaze. To crush fennel seeds, place them on a cutting board and rock the bottom edge of a skillet over them until they crack. To make a balsamic glaze, simmer ¼ cup balsamic vinegar and 2 tablespoons brown sugar in a small saucepan set over medium heat until slightly thickened, about 3 minutes.

1   Using highest sauté function, cook 1 tablespoon oil, garlic, and fennel seeds in Instant Pot until fragrant and garlic is light-golden brown, about 3 minutes. Stir in tomatoes and reserved juice and table salt. Lock lid in place and close pressure release valve. Select high pressure cook function and cook for 2 minutes.

2   Turn off Instant Pot and quick-release pressure. Carefully remove lid, allowing steam to escape away from you. Continue to cook tomato mixture using highest sauté function until sauce is slightly thickened, about 5 minutes.

3   Place burrata on plate and cut into rough 1½-inch pieces, collecting creamy liquid. Toss fennel and arugula with remaining 1 tablespoon oil in large bowl. Season with table salt and pepper to taste. Arrange toasts on individual serving plates and top with tomato mixture, fennel-arugula salad, and burrata and any accumulated liquid. Drizzle with glaze and extra oil, and sprinkle with sea salt. Serve.

per serving
Cal 540; Total Fat 31g; Sat Fat 10g; Chol 40mg; Sodium 1190mg; Total Carbs 53g, Fiber 4g, Total Sugar 10g; Added Sugar 0g; Protein 20g

individual asparagus and goat cheese frittatas

serves 4   **total time** 1 hour

- 1 tablespoon extra-virgin olive oil

- 8 ounces asparagus, trimmed and sliced ¼ inch thick

- 1 red bell pepper, stemmed, seeded, and chopped

- 2 shallots, minced

- 2 ounces goat cheese, crumbled (½ cup)

- 1 tablespoon minced fresh tarragon

- 1 teaspoon grated lemon zest

- 8 large eggs

- ½ teaspoon table salt

why this recipe works A vegetable-packed frittata makes for a satisfying light meal. Using individual ramekins as the cooking vessel allowed for easy transfer for serving (not to mention elegant presentation). We added a little water to our egg mixture to keep the frittatas tender, and sautéed a vibrant mix of vegetables to drive off their excess moisture and make sure they were fully cooked. Tangy goat cheese, tarragon, and lemon zest kept the frittatas bright. You will need four 6-ounce ramekins for this recipe. If using a 6-quart Instant Pot, arrange 3 ramekins on the trivet in step 2, then stack the fourth ramekin on top in the center. The bottom frittatas may puff up slightly around the base of the ramekin on top. To make this a heartier meal, serve with a salad and crusty bread.

1   Using highest sauté function, heat oil in Instant Pot until shimmering. Add asparagus, bell pepper, and shallots; cook until softened, about 5 minutes. Turn off Instant Pot and transfer vegetables to bowl. Stir in goat cheese, tarragon, and lemon zest.

2   Arrange trivet included with Instant Pot in base of now-empty insert and add 1 cup water. Spray four 6-ounce ramekins with vegetable oil spray. Beat eggs, ¼ cup water, and salt in large bowl until thoroughly combined. Divide vegetable mixture between prepared ramekins, then pour egg mixture over top (you may have some left over). Set ramekins on trivet. Lock lid in place and close pressure release valve. Select high pressure cook function and cook for 10 minutes.

3   Turn off Instant Pot and quick-release pressure. Carefully remove lid, allowing steam to escape away from you. Using tongs, transfer ramekins to wire rack and let cool slightly. Run paring knife around inside edge of ramekins to loosen frittatas, then invert onto individual serving plates. Serve.

per serving
Cal 240; Total Fat 16g; Sat Fat 6g; Chol 380mg; Sodium 500mg; Total Carbs 6g, Fiber 2g, Total Sugar 3g; Added Sugar 0g; Protein 17g

braised cabbage with pancetta, garlic, and parmesan

serves 4   **total time** 45 minutes

1 large head green cabbage (3 pounds)

4 ounces pancetta, chopped fine

6 garlic cloves, sliced thin

4 anchovy fillets, rinsed, patted dry, and minced

¼–½ teaspoon red pepper flakes

½ cup chicken broth

¼ teaspoon table salt

¼ cup chopped fresh parsley

2 tablespoons capers, rinsed and minced

1 teaspoon lemon juice

Extra-virgin olive oil

Grated Parmesan cheese

why this recipe works Cabbage isn't necessarily the first ingredient you reach for when you want to make a comforting meal, but when cooked under pressure it transforms into something meltingly tender and sweet. What's more, when cooked with fat, the sweet liquor it exudes will emulsify into a rich, smooth broth. We know of no fat more flavorful and savory than that rendered from pancetta. Anchovies, garlic, capers, and Parmesan further bolstered the umami of the dish. We saved the little nuggets of cooked pancetta to add at the end so they didn't lose their crunch during cooking. Bacon can be used in place of the pancetta. Serve with crusty bread or Garlic Toasts (page 19).

1 Cut cabbage into quarters, then cut away hard piece of core attached to each quarter. Slice each quarter crosswise into 1-inch-thick pieces; set aside.

2 Using highest sauté function, cook pancetta in Instant Pot, stirring often, until browned and fat is well rendered, 6 to 10 minutes. Using slotted spoon, transfer pancetta to paper towel-lined plate; set aside for serving.

3 Add garlic, anchovies, and pepper flakes to fat left in pot and cook, using highest sauté function, until fragrant, about 30 seconds. Stir in cabbage, broth, and salt. Lock lid in place and close pressure release valve. Select high pressure cook function and cook for 3 minutes.

4 Turn off Instant Pot and quick-release pressure. Carefully remove lid, allowing steam to escape away from you. Stir in parsley, capers, and lemon juice, and season with salt and pepper to taste. Drizzle individual portions with oil and sprinkle with pancetta and Parmesan. Serve.

per serving
Cal 220; Total Fat 9g; Sat Fat 3g; Chol 25mg; Sodium 1100mg; Total Carbs 22g, Fiber 9g, Total Sugar 12g; Added Sugar 0g; Protein 12g

garlicky kale and parsnips with soft-cooked eggs and pickled onions

serves 4   **total time** 45 minutes

- 12 ounces parsnips, peeled

- 2 tablespoons extra-virgin olive oil, plus extra for drizzling

- 4 garlic cloves, minced

- 2 pounds kale, stemmed and cut into 1-inch pieces

- ¾ cup chicken or vegetable broth

- ½ teaspoon table salt

- 4 large eggs

- ¼ cup Quick Pickled Onions (page 19)

- ½ cup Lemon-Yogurt Sauce (page 18)

- 1 teaspoon ground dried Aleppo pepper

why this recipe works We love kale for its savory heartiness. However, its fibrous texture means it needs lengthy cooking or a briefer but laborious two-step cooking process (usually blanching in boiling water and then finishing in a skillet). In the Instant Pot it just needed to be briefly wilted before going under pressure until tender. We added some sweet parsnips to offset the mild, appealing bitterness of the kale. To tie everything together we added easy-peel soft-cooked eggs for their oozy yolks and topped it all off with some sweet-sour pickled onions. If you can't find ground dried Aleppo pepper, you can substitute ½ teaspoon paprika and ¼ teaspoon finely chopped red pepper flakes. If cooking the eggs for 2½ minutes in step 3, we recommend using a kitchen timer to track the cook time once the Instant Pot has reached pressure. Serve with crusty bread or Garlic Toasts (page 19).

1 Cut parsnips into 2-inch lengths. Leave thin pieces whole, halve medium pieces lengthwise, and quarter thick pieces lengthwise. Using highest sauté function, cook oil and garlic in Instant Pot until fragrant, about 1 minute. Stir in half of kale and cook until slightly wilted, about 1 minute. Add remaining kale and repeat. Stir in broth and salt, then add parsnips. Lock lid in place and close pressure release valve. Select high pressure cook function and cook for 3 minutes.

2 Turn off Instant Pot and quick-release pressure. Carefully remove lid, allowing steam to escape away from you. Season kale and parsnips with salt and pepper to taste. Transfer to bowl and cover to keep warm. Discard cooking liquid in pot.

3 Arrange trivet included with Instant Pot in base of now-empty insert and add 1 cup water. Using highest sauté function, bring water to boil. Set eggs on trivet. Lock lid in place and close pressure release valve. Select high pressure cook function and set cook time for 3 minutes. Cook eggs for 2½ minutes (fully set whites with runny yolks) or 3 minutes (fully set whites with fudgy yolks).

Turn off Instant Pot and quick-release pressure. Carefully remove lid, allowing steam to escape away from you. Using tongs, transfer eggs to separate bowl and place under cold running water for 30 seconds. Drain and peel eggs.

4 Divide kale and parsnips among individual serving bowls. Top with pickled onions, yogurt sauce, and eggs. Sprinkle with Aleppo pepper and drizzle with extra oil. Serve.

per serving
Cal 330; Total Fat 15g; Sat Fat 3.5g; Chol 190mg; Sodium 600mg; Total Carbs 39g, Fiber 10g, Total Sugar 15g; Added Sugar 4g; Protein 16g

braised fennel with radicchio, pear, and pecorino

serves 4   **total time** 45 minutes

6 tablespoons extra-virgin olive oil, divided

2 fennel bulbs (12 ounces each), 2 tablespoons fronds chopped, stalks discarded, bulbs halved, each half cut into 1-inch-thick wedges

¾ teaspoon table salt, divided

½ teaspoon grated lemon zest plus 4 teaspoons juice

5 ounces (5 cups) baby arugula

1 small head radicchio (6 ounces), shredded

1 Bosc or Bartlett pear, quartered, cored, and sliced thin

¼ cup whole almonds, toasted and chopped

Shaved Pecorino Romano cheese

why this recipe works When fennel is cooked under pressure, its sharpness mellows into something sweeter and almost caramelized—a perfect companion to a mix of contrasting bitter greens and sweet pear to make a salad worthy of an upscale brunch spread. We started by cutting the fennel into wedges and browning them in the Instant Pot before cooking them under pressure for a mere 2 minutes. We whisked together a lemony dressing, assembled the salad, and topped it off with salty Pecorino Romano and toasty, crunchy almonds. Don't core the fennel before cutting it into wedges; the core helps hold the wedges together during cooking. To make this a heartier meal, add Hard- or Soft-Cooked Eggs (page 10) and serve with crusty bread.

1   Using highest sauté function, heat 2 tablespoons oil in Instant Pot for 5 minutes (or until just smoking). Brown half of fennel, about 3 minutes per side; transfer to plate. Repeat with 1 tablespoon oil and remaining fennel; do not remove from pot.

2   Return first batch of fennel to pot along with ½ cup water and ½ teaspoon salt. Lock lid in place and close pressure release valve. Select high pressure cook function and cook for 2 minutes. Turn off Instant Pot and quick-release pressure. Carefully remove lid, allowing steam to escape away from you. Using slotted spoon, transfer fennel to plate; discard cooking liquid.

3   Whisk remaining 3 tablespoons oil, lemon zest and juice, and remaining ¼ teaspoon salt together in large bowl. Add arugula, radicchio, and pear and toss to coat. Transfer arugula mixture to serving dish and arrange fennel wedges on top. Sprinkle with almonds, fennel fronds, and Pecorino. Serve.

per serving
Cal 290; Total Fat 26g; Sat Fat 3.5g; Chol 0mg; Sodium 300mg; Total Carbs 22g, Fiber 7g, Total Sugar 11g; Added Sugar 0g; Protein 5g

green beans with potatoes and basil

serves 4 **total time** 1 hour

2 tablespoons extra-virgin olive oil, plus extra for drizzling

1 onion, chopped fine

2 tablespoons minced fresh oregano or 2 teaspoons dried

2 tablespoons tomato paste

4 garlic cloves, minced

1 (14.5-ounce) can whole peeled tomatoes, drained with juice reserved, chopped

1 cup water

1 teaspoon table salt

¼ teaspoon pepper

1½ pounds green beans, trimmed and cut into 2-inch lengths

1 pound Yukon Gold potatoes, peeled and cut into 1-inch pieces

3 tablespoons chopped fresh basil or parsley

2 tablespoons toasted pine nuts

Shaved Parmesan cheese

why this recipe works Unlike crisp-tender green beans that have been steamed or sautéed, Greece's traditional braised green beans boast a uniquely soft texture without being mushy. Unfortunately, achieving this can require 2 hours of simmering. To get ultratender braised green beans in a fraction of the time, we loved the quick-cooking, even heat of the Instant Pot. For a more substantial meal, we added chunks of potatoes, which turned tender in the same amount of time as the beans. Canned tomatoes supplied a sweetness, while their juice along with a little water provided just enough braising liquid for the beans. Shaved Parmesan, a final drizzle of fruity extra-virgin olive oil, and toasted pine nuts added richness and textural contrast. To make this a heartier meal, add Hard- or Soft-Cooked Eggs (page 10) and serve with crusty bread.

1 Using highest sauté function, heat oil in Instant Pot until shimmering. Add onion and cook until softened, about 5 minutes. Stir in oregano, tomato paste, and garlic and cook until fragrant, about 30 seconds. Stir in tomatoes and their juice, water, salt, and pepper, then stir in green beans and potatoes. Lock lid in place and close pressure release valve. Select high pressure cook function and cook for 5 minutes.

2 Turn off Instant Pot and quick-release pressure. Carefully remove lid, allowing steam to escape away from you. Season with salt and pepper to taste. Sprinkle individual portions with basil, pine nuts, and Parmesan and drizzle with extra oil. Serve.

per serving
Cal 280; Total Fat 10g; Sat Fat 1.5g; Chol 0mg; Sodium 880mg; Total Carbs 42g, Fiber 8g, Total Sugar 11g; Added Sugar 0g; Protein 7g

braised radishes with sugar snap peas and dukkah

serves 4   **total time** 45 minutes

- ¼ cup extra-virgin olive oil, divided
- 1 shallot, sliced thin
- 3 garlic cloves, sliced thin
- 1½ pounds radishes, 2 cups greens reserved, radishes trimmed and halved if small or quartered if large
- ½ cup water
- ½ teaspoon table salt
- 8 ounces sugar snap peas, strings removed, sliced thin on bias
- 8 ounces cremini mushrooms, trimmed and sliced thin
- 2 teaspoons grated lemon zest plus 1 teaspoon juice
- 1 cup plain Greek yogurt
- ½ cup fresh cilantro leaves
- 3 tablespoons dukkah

why this recipe works Cooking a radish transforms it from a peppery and crisp salad component to a sweeter, meatier spring vegetable. To build a flavorful braising liquid, we softened shallot and garlic in oil before adding some bright lemon zest and water. We loved the pairing of thinly sliced sugar snap peas for their vegetal sweetness and slight crunch. We found a brief stint in the residual heat of the cooked radishes was enough to take away the snap peas' raw texture while retaining their freshness, and thinly sliced mushrooms stirred in at the end added heft. Some creamy Greek yogurt and *dukkah,* the Egyptian spice blend, turned it into a complete meal. If your radishes do not come with greens, substitute baby arugula. We prefer to make our own Dukkah (page 19), but any store-bought variety will work.

1 Using highest sauté function, heat 2 tablespoons oil in Instant Pot until shimmering. Add shallot and cook until softened, about 2 minutes. Stir in garlic and cook until fragrant, about 30 seconds. Stir in radishes, water, and salt. Lock lid in place and close pressure release valve. Select high pressure cook function and cook for 1 minute.

2 Turn off Instant Pot and quick-release pressure. Carefully remove lid, allowing steam to escape away from you. Stir in snap peas, cover, and let sit until heated through, about 3 minutes. Add radish greens, mushrooms, lemon zest and juice, and remaining 2 tablespoons oil and gently toss to combine. Season with salt and pepper to taste.

3 Spread ¼ cup yogurt over bottom of 4 individual serving plates. Using slotted spoon, arrange vegetable mixture on top and sprinkle with cilantro and dukkah. Serve.

per serving
Cal 310; Total Fat 23g; Sat Fat 8g; Chol 10mg; Sodium 320mg; Total Carbs 17g, Fiber 5g, Total Sugar 9g; Added Sugar 0g; Protein 10g

spiced winter squash with halloumi and shaved brussels sprouts

serves 4   **total time** 1 hour

- 3 tablespoons extra-virgin olive oil, divided
- 2 tablespoons lemon juice
- 2 garlic cloves, minced, divided
- ⅛ teaspoon plus ½ teaspoon table salt, divided
- 8 ounces Brussels sprouts, trimmed, halved, and sliced very thin
- 1 (8-ounce) block halloumi cheese, sliced crosswise into ¾-inch-thick slabs
- 4 scallions, white parts minced, green parts sliced thin on bias
- ½ teaspoon ground cardamom
- ¼ teaspoon ground cumin
- ⅛ teaspoon cayenne pepper
- 2 pounds butternut squash, peeled, seeded, and cut into 1-inch pieces (5 cups)
- ½ cup chicken or vegetable broth
- 2 teaspoons honey
- ¼ cup dried cherries
- 2 tablespoons roasted pepitas

why this recipe works Golden-crusted salty halloumi and velvety, sweet squash are a marriage of opposing textures and flavors. Halloumi is a brined cheese originally from Cyprus, with a semifirm, springy texture, and its high melting point allows it to retain its shape when cooked. Sautéing it yielded a crispy exterior to contrast with the creamy interior, and we used its rendered fat to bloom spices before adding scallion whites to create the base for the squash. In the Instant Pot, raw, hard cubes of squash were transformed into sweet, melting chunks that were quickly coaxed into a purée with a masher. A lemony Brussels sprouts salad both provided acidity to offset the squash's sweetness as well as crunch against its silky texture. A little drizzle of honey accentuated the mild tang of the salty cheese, and chewy dried cherries and roasted pepitas brought textural contrast with a bit of sweetness. Look for Brussels sprouts with small, tight heads that are no more than 1½ inches in diameter, as they're likely to be sweeter and more tender than larger sprouts.

1   Whisk 1 tablespoon oil, lemon juice, ¼ teaspoon garlic, and ⅛ teaspoon salt together in bowl. Add Brussels sprouts and toss to coat; let sit until ready to serve.

2   Using highest sauté function, heat remaining 2 tablespoons oil in Instant Pot until shimmering. Arrange halloumi around edges of pot and cook until browned, about 3 minutes per side; transfer to plate. Add scallion whites to fat left in pot and cook until softened, about 2 minutes. Stir in remaining garlic, cardamom, cumin, and cayenne and cook until fragrant, about 30 seconds. Stir in squash, broth, and remaining ½ teaspoon salt. Lock lid in place and close pressure release valve. Select high pressure cook function and cook for 6 minutes.

3 Turn off Instant Pot and quick-release pressure. Carefully remove lid, allowing steam to escape away from you. Using highest sauté function, continue to cook squash mixture, stirring occasionally until liquid is almost completely evaporated, about 5 minutes. Turn off Instant Pot. Using potato masher, mash squash until mostly smooth. Season with salt and pepper to taste.

4 Spread portion of squash over bottom of individual serving plates. Top with Brussels sprouts and halloumi. Drizzle with honey and sprinkle with cherries, pepitas, and scallion greens. Serve.

per serving
Cal 470; Total Fat 28g; Sat Fat 12g; Chol 45mg; Sodium 1060mg; Total Carbs 40g, Fiber 7g, Total Sugar 13g; Added Sugar 3g; Protein 18g

braised whole cauliflower with north african spices

serves 4   **total time** 45 minutes

2 tablespoons extra-virgin olive oil

6 garlic cloves, minced

3 anchovy fillets, rinsed and minced (optional)

2 teaspoons ras el hanout

⅛ teaspoon red pepper flakes

1 (28-ounce) can whole peeled tomatoes, drained with juice reserved, chopped coarse

1 large head cauliflower (3 pounds)

½ cup pitted brine-cured green olives, chopped coarse

¼ cup golden raisins

¼ cup fresh cilantro leaves

¼ cup pine nuts, toasted

why this recipe works Whole braised cauliflower is a showstopper and, when done in the Instant Pot, a snap to make. We started by making an intensely savory cooking liquid of garlic, anchovies, *ras el hanout*, and tomatoes. When cauliflower's fibrous core didn't always cook through during testing, we made deep cuts in the stem to allow the liquid and heat to reach the center, which rendered the whole head perfectly tender. After releasing the pressure, we removed the cauliflower, stirred in the sweet-savory combo of raisins and olives, and thickened the sauce before spooning it over the beautiful vegetable. You can find ras el hanout in the spice aisle of most well-stocked supermarkets. Serve with rice, grains, or crusty bread.

1 Using highest sauté function, cook oil, garlic, anchovies (if using), ras el hanout, and pepper flakes in Instant Pot until fragrant, about 3 minutes. Turn off Instant Pot, then stir in tomatoes and reserved juice.

2 Trim outer leaves of cauliflower and cut stem flush with bottom florets. Using paring knife, cut 4-inch-deep cross in stem. Nestle cauliflower stem side down into pot and spoon some of sauce over top. Lock lid in place and close pressure release valve. Select high pressure cook function and cook for 3 minutes.

3 Turn off Instant Pot and quick-release pressure. Carefully remove lid, allowing steam to escape away from you. Using tongs and slotted spoon, transfer cauliflower to serving dish and tent with aluminum foil. Stir olives and raisins into sauce and cook, using highest sauté function, until sauce has thickened slightly, about 5 minutes. Season with salt and pepper to taste. Cut cauliflower into wedges and spoon some of sauce over top. Sprinkle with cilantro and pine nuts. Serve, passing remaining sauce separately.

per serving
Cal 340; Total Fat 15g; Sat Fat 2g; Chol 5mg; Sodium 1090mg; Total Carbs 44g, Fiber 11g, Total Sugar 24g; Added Sugar 0g; Protein 12g

ratatouille

serves 4   **total time** 1 hour

- 2 tablespoons extra-virgin olive oil

- 2 red or yellow bell peppers, stemmed, seeded, and cut into 1-inch pieces

- 1 onion, chopped fine

- 1 teaspoon table salt

- 4 garlic cloves, minced

- 1 teaspoon herbes de Provence

- ¼ teaspoon red pepper flakes

- 1 (28-ounce) can whole peeled tomatoes, drained with juice reserved, chopped

- 1 pound eggplant, cut into ½-inch pieces

- 1 pound zucchini, quartered lengthwise and sliced 1 inch thick

- 1 tablespoon sherry vinegar

- ¼ cup basil pesto, plus extra for serving

why this recipe works The Instant Pot is tailor-made for traditionally long-cooked stews, but this Provençal standby is chock-full of watery vegetables, and the Instant Pot doesn't allow for any evaporation—a recipe for bland, runny ratatouille. We wanted perfectly cooked vegetables in a liquid with a saucy, not thin and soupy, consistency. Sautéing the peppers released some of their moisture and concentrated their flavor, and we found that pretreating the eggplant wasn't necessary—cutting it small ensured it would break down and help create a thicker sauce (it also helped shorten the cooking time). Canned whole tomatoes and zucchini rounded out the vegetable medley. Garlic, pepper flakes, and herbes de Provence added spice and characteristic backbone. A splash of vinegar helped wake up the flavors of the sweet vegetables after releasing the pressure, and bright pesto brought a fresh, rich finish. We prefer to make our own Classic Basil Pesto (page 16), but any store-bought variety will work. Serve with rice, grains, or crusty bread.

1 Using highest sauté function, heat oil in Instant Pot until shimmering. Add bell peppers, onion, and salt and cook until vegetables are softened, about 5 minutes. Stir in garlic, herbes de Provence, and pepper flakes and cook until fragrant, about 30 seconds. Stir in tomatoes and reserved juice, eggplant, and zucchini. Lock lid in place and close pressure release valve. Select high pressure cook function and cook for 1 minute.

2 Turn off Instant Pot and quick-release pressure. Carefully remove lid, allowing steam to escape away from you. Using highest sauté function, continue to cook vegetable mixture until zucchini is tender and sauce has thickened slightly, 3 to 5 minutes. Stir in vinegar and season with salt and pepper to taste. Dollop individual portions with pesto and serve, passing extra pesto separately.

per serving
Cal 290; Total Fat 19g; Sat Fat 3g; Chol 0mg; Sodium 920mg; Total Carbs 24g, Fiber 7g, Total Sugar 13g; Added Sugar 0g; Protein 6g

conversions and equivalents

Some say cooking is a science and an art. We would say that geography has a hand in it, too. Flours and sugars manufactured in the United Kingdom and elsewhere will feel and taste different from those manufactured in the United States. So we cannot promise that the loaf of bread you bake in Canada or England will taste the same as a loaf baked in the States, but we can offer guidelines for converting weights and measures. We also recommend that you rely on your instincts when making our recipes. Refer to the visual cues provided. If the dough hasn't "come together in a ball" as described, you may need to add more flour—even if the recipe doesn't tell you to. You be the judge.

The recipes in this book were developed using standard U.S. measures following U.S. government guidelines. The charts below offer equivalents for U.S. and metric measures. All conversions are approximate and have been rounded up or down to the nearest whole number.

example

1 teaspoon = 4.9292 milliliters, rounded up to 5 milliliters

1 ounce = 28.3495 grams, rounded down to 28 grams

volume conversions

u.s.	metric
1 teaspoon	5 milliliters
2 teaspoons	10 milliliters
1 tablespoon	15 milliliters
2 tablespoons	30 milliliters
¼ cup	59 milliliters
⅓ cup	79 milliliters
½ cup	118 milliliters
¾ cup	177 milliliters
1 cup	237 milliliters
1¼ cups	296 milliliters
1½ cups	355 milliliters
2 cups (1 pint)	473 milliliters
2½ cups	591 milliliters
3 cups	710 milliliters
4 cups (1 quart)	0.946 liter
1.06 quarts	1 liter
4 quarts (1 gallon)	3.8 liters

weight conversions

ounces	grams
½	14
¾	21
1	28
1½	43
2	57
2½	71
3	85
3½	99
4	113
4½	128
5	142
6	170
7	198
8	227
9	255
10	283
12	340
16 (1 pound)	454

index

Note: Page references in *italics* indicate photographs.